All-American Afghans
Crochet ™

Edited by Laura Scott

HOUSE of
WHITE
BIRCHES
PUBLISHERS
SINCE 1947

All-American Crochet Afghans

Editor: Laura Scott
Associate Editor: Cathy Reef
Design Manager: Vicki Blizzard
Technical Editor: Agnes Russell
Copy Editors: Mary Martin, Nicki Lehman
Publications Coordinator: Tanya Turner

Photography: Tammy Christian, Jeff Chilcote, Kelly Heydinger, Justin P. Wiard
Photography Assistant: Linda Quinlan

Production Coordinator: Brenda Gallmeyer
Book Design: Jessi Butler
Cover Design: Jessi Butler
Production Artist: Pam Gregory
Production Assistants: Janet Bowers, Marj Morgan
Technical Artists: Leslie Brandt, Julie Catey, Chad Summers
Traffic Coordinator: Sandra Beres

Publishers: Carl H. Muselman, Arthur K. Muselman
Chief Executive Officer: John Robinson
Marketing Director: Scott Moss
Book Marketing Manager: Craig Scott
Product Development Director: Vivian Rothe
Publishing Services Manager: Brenda R. Wendling

Printed in the United States of America
First Printing: 2001
Library of Congress Number: 00-112314
ISBN: 1-882138-77-5

A Note From The Editor

Several years ago, I met an interesting woman who mentioned she enjoyed traveling. I assumed she meant international travel so I asked her what countries she had visited. I was surprised when she replied, "Oh no. I just travel in the United States. I figure we have more to see in this country than many parts of the world!"

Her words came back to me as I thought about this book. We do live in an amazingly diverse country. We have thick forests and green meadows, grand canyons and grassy plains, rolling hills and majestic mountains, lush farmland and lonely deserts, Atlantic waves and Pacific beaches. The beauty and variety of landscape in this country is unparalleled the world over!

Instead of just another book of crocheted afghans, my staff and I wanted to bring you something a little different. With this in mind, we've divided this book into eight chapters, with each chapter representing a different region of this great country we call America. From Maine to California, you'll find afghans to represent the best of what each region of out country offers.

So sit back, and take a cross-country journey as you explore this collection of All-American afghans!

Laura Scott

Editor, *All-American Crochet Afghans*

Contents

New England Beauty

Cottage gardens with picket fences, white-steepled churches, and rolling hills dappled with a rainbow of color—these are just a few sights of beautiful New England. Bring a sampling of its beauty into your home with this collection of keepsake afghans!

American Pride

Crochet this patriotic afghan to bring back memories of small-town parades held every Fourth of July! Invite your crocheting friends to stitch and join motifs with you!

Design by Katherine Eng

SKILL LEVEL: Beginner

SIZE: 41 x 62 inches

MATERIALS

- Coats & Clark Red Heart Super Saver worsted weight yarn: 15½ oz soft navy #387, 9½ oz soft white #316, 4 oz cherry red #319, 3 oz royal blue #385, 2½ oz light periwinkle #347, 2 oz skipper blue #384
- Size H/8 crochet hook or size needed to obtain gauge
- Size G/6 crochet hook
- Yarn needle

GAUGE

Rnds 1 and 2 = 3 inches; Square = 5½ inches

Check gauge to save time.

PATTERN NOTES

Weave in loose ends as work progresses.

Join rnds with a sl st unless otherwise stated.

Rnd 4 is crocheted in 3 different shades of blue; make 27 light periwinkle, 22 with skipper blue and 28 with royal blue.

PATTERN STITCHES

Shell: [2 dc, ch 2, 2 dc] in indicated st.

Beg shell: [Ch 3, dc, ch 2, 2 dc] in indicated st.

SQUARE

(Make 77)

Rnd 1 (RS): With crochet hook size H and cherry red, ch 4, sl st to join to form a ring, ch 1, [sc in ring, ch 3] 7 times, sc in ring, ch 1, hdc in beg sc to form last ch sp, turn. (8 ch-3 sps)

Rnd 2 (WS): Ch 1, sc in same sp as beg ch-1, [ch 3, sc in next ch-3 sp] 7 times, ch 3, join in beg sc, fasten off, turn. (8 ch-3 sps)

Rnd 3 (RS): Draw up a lp of white in any ch-3 sp, ch 1, sc in same ch-3 sp, [5 dc in next sc, sc in next ch-3 sp] 7 times, 5 dc in next sc, join in beg sc, fasten off. (8 groups 5-dc; 8 sc)

Rnd 4 (RS): With royal blue (light periwinkle or skipper blue) as indicated, draw up a lp in center dc of any 5-dc group, ch 1, sc in same dc as beg ch-1, *ch 2, dc in next sc, ch 2, shell in center dc of next 5-dc group, ch 2, dc in next sc, ch 2 **, sc in center dc of next 5-dc group, rep from * around, ending last rep at **, join in beg sc, fasten off. (4 corner shells)

Rnd 5 (RS): Draw up a lp of soft navy in first ch-2 sp to the left of any corner, ch 1, 2 sc in same ch-2 sp, *[ch 1, 2 sc in next ch-2 sp] 3 times, ch 1, sk 1 dc, sc in next dc, [sc, ch 3, sc] in next corner ch-2 sp, sc in next dc, ch 1, sk 1 dc **, 2 sc in next ch-2 sp, rep from * around, ending last rep at **, join in beg sc, fasten off.

ASSEMBLY

Arrange squares in 7 rows of 11 squares. Rows 1, 4 and 7 alternate from top to bottom, royal blue and light periwinkle. Rows 2 and 6 alternate top to bottom, light periwinkle and skipper blue. Rows 3 and 5 alternate top to bottom,

Continued on page 26

Painted Stripes

*Long, elegant panels worked with warm
colors and creamy white make this afghan
a treat for the eyes as well as soothing for the body.*

Design by Tammy Hildebrand

SKILL LEVEL: Intermediate

SIZE: 41 x 63 inches

MATERIALS
- Coats & Clark Red Heart Super Saver worsted weight yarn: 14 oz painted desert print #303 (MC), 8 oz Windsor blue #380 (A), 8 oz country rose #374 (B)
- Coats & Clark Red Heart Classic worsted weight yarn: 8 oz teal #48 (C), 12 oz eggshell #111 (D)
- Size J/10 crochet hook or size needed to obtain gauge
- Tapestry needle

GAUGE
Strip width = 5½ inches; 3 dc = 1 inch

Check gauge to save time.

PATTERN NOTES
Weave in loose ends as work progresses.

Sl st to join each rnd in top of beg st.

PATTERN STITCH
Joining: Sc, ch 1, drop lp from hook, insert hook in center ch of corresponding ch-3 sp on previous panel, pick up dropped lp and draw through, ch 1, sc in same st on working panel.

PANEL CENTER
(Make 7)

Note: *Make 2 each with B and C and 3 with A.*

Row 1 (RS): Ch 153, dc in 4th ch from hook, dc in each rem ch across, fasten off. (151 dc)

PANEL
Rnd 1 (RS): Attach MC with sc in first st of panel center, fpdc around next st, [sc in next st, fpdc in next st] 74 times, sc in next st, work 7 sc over post of last st, working in bottom lps of base ch, [sc in next st, fpdc around next st] 74 times, sc in next st, work 7 sc over post of first st, join in beg sc, fasten off.

Rnd 2 (RS): Working in back lps for this rnd only, attach D with sl st in center sc at either end of panel, ch 3 (counts as first dc throughout), dc in same st, 2 dc in each of next 2 sts, dc in each of next 153 sts, 2 dc in each of next 5 sts, dc in each of next 153 sts, 2 dc in each of next 2 sts, join in top of beg ch-3, fasten off.

Rnd 3 (RS): Working with same color as panel center, attach with sc in first st of center 2-st group at either end of panel, sc in next 5 sts, *ch 1, [fpdc in next st, ch 1, sk next st] 76 times, ch 1, sk next st *, sc in next 10 sts, rep from * to *, sc in each of next 4 sts, join in beg sc, fasten off.

Rnd 4 (RS): Attach MC with sc in first st of 10 sc at either end of panel, sc in next 9 sts, *working over ch-1 sps of previous rnd, in skipped sts, [dc in next skipped st, sc in next fpdc] 76 times, dc in next skipped st *, sc in next 10 sts, rep from * to *, join in beg sc, fasten off.

Rnd 5 (RS): Working in back lps for this rnd only, attach D with sl st in first st of 10 sc at either end of panel, ch 3, dc in each of next 2 sts, 2 dc in each of next 4 sts, dc in each of next 159 sts, 2 dc in each of next 4 sts, dc in each of next 156 sts, join in top of beg ch-3, fasten off.

Note: *The following Rnd 6 is worked around the first panel only.*

Rnd 6 (RS): Working on first panel only, attach MC with sc in first dc of first 2-st group at either end of panel, ch 1, [sc in next st, ch 1] 10 times, [{sc, ch 3} in next st, sk next st] 76 times, [sc in next st, ch 1] 17 times, [{sc, ch 3} in next st, sk next st] 76 times, [sc in next st, ch 1] 6 times, join in beg sc, fasten off.

Note: *The following Rnd 6 is worked around rem panels, joining working panel to previous panel along 1 edge.*

Rnd 6 (RS): Attach MC with sc in first dc of first 2-st group at either end of panel, ch 1, [sc in next st, ch 1] 10 times, [work joining, sk next st] 76 times, [sc in next st, ch 1] 17 times, [{sc, ch 3} in next st, sk next st] 76 times, [sc in next st, ch 1] 6 times, join in beg sc, fasten off. ★

All-American Plaid

Worked on a double-ended crochet hook, this gorgeous afghan is as handsome on one side as it is on the other! Work it in the colors shown for patriotic pride!

Design by Darla Fanton

SKILL LEVEL: Intermediate

SIZE: 52 x 72 inches

MATERIALS

- Coats & Clark Red Heart Super Saver worsted weight yarn: 10 oz soft navy #387, 9 oz each burgundy #376 and cherry red #319, 8 oz gold #321, 6 oz cornmeal #320
- Coats & Clark Red Heart Classic worsted weight yarn: 9 oz skipper blue #848
- Susan Bates size K/10½ double-ended crochet hook or size needed to obtain gauge
- Sizes J/10 and K/10½ crochet hooks
- Tapestry needle

GAUGE

4 sts = 1 inch; 4 rows = 1 inch
Check gauge to save time.

PATTERN NOTES

Weave in loose ends as work progresses.

If you have difficulty keeping all of the sts on the hook, cap the unused end of hook with either a knitting needle protector or a clean wine cork.

When picking up a lp in horizontal st, insert hook under top lp only.

Carry unused yarn short distances along side edge by bringing it to the front and working over it for beg ch-1 on odd-numbered rows. Do not carry yarn over more than 4 rows.

AFGHAN

Row 1: With soft navy, ch 186, working through back lps only, insert hook in 2nd ch from hook, yo and draw through, [draw up a lp in next ch] 4 times, *[sk next 2 chs, yo twice, draw up lp in each of next 3 chs] 3 times, [draw up lp in next ch] 12 times, rep from * across foundation ch, ending [draw up lp in next ch] 3 times, slide all sts to opposite end of hook, turn. (186 lps on hook.

Row 2: To work lps off hook, place burgundy on hook with sl knot, working from left to right, draw through first lp, *yo, draw through 2 lps (1 lp of each color), rep from * across until 1 lp rem on hook, do not turn.

Row 3: With burgundy and working right to left, ch 1, sk first vertical bar, [draw up a lp in next horizontal st] 5 times, *[sk next 3 vertical bars, yo twice, pick up a lp in each of next 3 horizontal sts] 3 times, [draw up a lp in next horizontal st] 12 times, rep from * across, ending [draw up a lp in next horizontal st] 3 times, slide all sts to opposite end of hook, turn. (186 lps on hook)

Row 4: Pick up soft navy, yo and draw through 1 lp, *yo and draw through 2 lps (1 of each color), rep from * until 1 lp rem on hook, do not turn.

Row 5: With soft navy, rep Row 3.

Row 6: With burgundy, rep Row 4.

Row 7: Rep Row 3.

Rows 8 & 9: With blue, rep Rows 2 and 3.

Rows 10 & 11: With cherry red, rep Rows 2 and 3.

Row 12: With blue, rep Row 4.

Row 13: With blue, rep Row 3.

Row 14: With cherry red, rep Row 4.

Rows 15–18: Rep Rows 11–14.

Row 19: Rep Row 11.

Rows 20 & 21: With gold, rep Rows 2 and 3.

Rows 22 & 23: With cornmeal, rep Rows 2 and 3.

Rows 24–26: Rep Rows 12–14.

Rows 27–30: Rep Rows 11–14.

Rows 31–34: Rep Rows 11–14.

Row 35: Rep Row 11.

Row 36: With soft navy, rep Row 2.

Row 37: Rep Row 5.

Rows 38–43: Rep Rows 2–7.

Rows 44–47: Rep Rows 20–23.

Rows 48–51: Rep Rows 4–7.

Rows 52–376: Rep Rows 4–51, ending last rep with a Row 40 pattern.

Row 377: With soft navy and working right to left, ch 1, sk first vertical bar, [insert hook in next horizontal st, yo and draw through st and lp on hook] 5 times, *[ch 2, sk next 3 vertical bars, draw up a lp in next horizontal st and draw through lp on hook] 3 times, [draw up a lp in next horizontal st and draw through lp on hook] 12 times, rep from * across, ending with [draw up a lp in next horizontal st and draw through lp on hook] 3 times, fasten off.

VERTICAL STRIPES

With predominantly blue side facing and beg at top edge, working over the yo lps, sc over each lp using the standard K hook, being careful to not draw the sc sts too tightly. For each set of 3

Continued on page 26

Painted Daisies

Bring the freshness and beauty of springtime blooms into your home with this enchanting afghan and pillow pair! If you look closely, you'll see the pink painted daisies in each motif!

Design by Kathryn Clark

SKILL LEVEL: Intermediate

SIZE

Afghan: 52 x 64 inches

Pillow: 12 inches in diameter plus trim

MATERIALS

- Caron Simply Soft worsted weight yarn (3 oz per skein): 2 skeins soft pink #2614 (A), 3 skeins English rose #2646 (B), 4 skeins white #2601 (C), 1 skein sage #2611 (D), 1 skein meadow #2636 (E) and 7 skeins fir #2618 (F)
- Size I/9 crochet hook or size needed to obtain gauge
- 12-inch round pillow form or ½ yd white material and fiberfill
- Yarn needle

GAUGE

Rnds 1 and 2 = 2¾ inches; side edge of triangle = 6 inches

Check gauge to save time.

PATTERN NOTES

Weave in loose ends as work progresses.

Join rnds with a sl st unless otherwise stated.

For smoother transitions, change colors just before drawing the last lp through of the preceding st.

Afghan

TRIANGLE 1
(Make 58)

Rnd 1 (RS): With A, ch 5, sl st to join to form a ring, ch 1, [sc in ring, ch 3] 6 times, join in beg sc. (6 ch-3 sps)

Rnd 2: Sl st into ch-3 sp, change to B, ch 1, *[sc, ch 1, dc, ch 1, sc] in ch-3 sp, ch 1, rep from * around, join in beg sc. (6 dc)

Rnd 3: Sl st into next dc, change to C, ch 1, *sc in dc, ch 3, sk next 2 sts, hdc in next ch-1 sp, ch 3, sk next 2 sts, sc in next dc, ch 3, sk next 2 sts, dc in next ch-1 sp, ch 3, sk next 2 sts, rep from * around, join in beg sc. (3 dc; 3 hdc; 6 sc)

Rnd 4: Sl st in next ch sp, ch 1, sc in same ch sp, ch 2, sc in next ch sp, *ch 2, [sc, hdc, dc, tr] in next ch sp, ch 4, dc in 3rd ch from hook, ch 2, sl st in same 3rd ch from hook, sc in next ch, [tr, dc, hdc, sc] in next ch sp, ch 2 *, [sc in next ch sp, ch 2] twice, change to D, [sc, hdc, dc, tr] in next ch sp, change to E, ch 4, dc in 3rd ch from hook, ch 2, sl st in same 3rd ch from hook, sc in next ch, [tr, dc, hdc, sc] in next ch sp, change to C, [ch 2, sc in next ch sp] twice, rep from * to *, join in beg sc, fasten off.

TRIANGLE 2
(Make 58)

Rnds 1–3: Rep Rnds 1–3 of Triangle 1.

Rnd 4: Sl st into next ch sp, ch 1, sc in same ch sp, ch 2, sc in next ch sp, *ch 2, [sc, hdc, dc, tr] in next ch sp, ch 4, dc in 3rd ch from hook, ch 2, sl st in same 3rd ch from hook, sc in next ch, [tr, dc, hdc, sc] in next ch sp, ch 2 *, [sc in next ch sp, ch 2] twice, change to E, [sc, hdc, dc, tr] in next ch sp, ch 4, dc in 3rd ch from hook, ch 2, sl st in same 3rd ch from hook, sc in next ch, change to D, [tr, dc, hdc, sc] in

next ch sp, change to C, [ch 2, sc in next ch sp] twice, rep from * to *, join in beg sc, fasten off.

TRIANGLE BORDER

Working counterclockwise around triangle, beg in desired corner, join F in dc, *[sc, ch 5, sc] in dc, ch 3, sk chs, hdc in next sc, ch 3, sk next 2 sts, sc in next hdc, [ch 3, sc in next ch sp] 3 times, ch 3, sc in next hdc, ch 3, sk next 2 sts, hdc in next ch, ch 3, rep from * around, join in beg sc, fasten off.

JOINING TRIANGLES

Taking care to position motifs so each side mirrors the opposing motif side, follow instructions for triangle border with the following changes for joining sides: Ch 2, sl st in 3rd ch of ch-5 sp of adjacent motif, ch 2 instead of ch 5; ch 1, sl st in 2nd ch of ch-3 sp of adjacent motif, ch 1 instead of ch 3.

Using Afghan Motif Placement diagram 1 as a guide, continue joining triangles as indicated.

AFGHAN BORDER

Rnd 1: Attach F in with *sc in joining st marked with • on Afghan Motif Placement diagram , [ch 3, sc in next ch sp] 20 times, ch 3, sc in joining st, †[ch 3, sc in next ch sp] 10 times, sc in next ch sp, [ch 3, sc in next ch sp] 9 times, ch 3, sc in joining st †, rep from † to †, [ch 3, sc in next ch sp] 20 times, ch 3, sc in joining st, [ch 3, sc in next ch sp] 60 times, ch 3, rep from *, join in beg sc.

Rnd 2: Sl st into ch sp, ch 1, sc in same sp, ch 3, [sc in next ch sp, ch 3] rep around with the following exception: do not ch-3 on

Continued on page 27

Christmas Crosses

Add warmth to your home, body and spirit with this inspirational Christmas afghan. Red and green crosses designed into the afghan make it extra special!

Design by Tammy Hildebrand

SKILL LEVEL: Intermediate

SIZE: 46 x 76½ inches

MATERIALS
- Coats & Clark Red Heart Light & Lofty textured yarn: 20 oz cloud #9311 (MC), 16 oz pine #9632 (A), 16 oz wine #9376 (B)
- Size K/10½ crochet hook or size needed to obtain gauge
- Tapestry needle

GAUGE
2 tr and 1 cross st = 4 inches; 4 rows = 3 inches
Check gauge to save time.

PATTERN NOTE
Weave in loose ends as work progresses.

AFGHAN
Row 1 (RS): With MC, ch 93, dc in 6th ch from hook, dc in next ch, ch 1, sk next ch, [dc in each of next 2 chs, ch 1, sk next ch] 28 times, dc in last ch, fasten off.

Row 2 (RS): Attach A with sl st in 4th ch of beg ch-5, ch 3 (counts as first dc throughout), working in skipped chs, over ch-1, tr in next skipped ch, sk next dc, dc in next dc, working over st just made, dc in skipped dc (cross st), tr in next skipped ch, [cross st over next 2 sts, tr in next skipped st] 28 times, dc in last st, fasten off.

Row 3 (RS): Attach MC with sl st in top of beg ch-3, ch 4 (counts as first dc, ch 1 throughout), sk next st, [dc in each of next 2 sts, ch 1, sk next st] 29 times, dc in last st, fasten off.

Row 4 (RS): Attach B with sl st in 3rd ch of beg ch-4, ch 3, working in skipped sts of previous row, over ch-1, tr in next skipped st, [work cross st over next 2 sts, tr in next skipped st] 29 times, dc in last st, fasten off.

Row 5 (RS): Rep Row 3.

Row 6 (RS): With A, rep Row 4.

[Rep Rows 3–6] 17 times. Rep Row 3, fasten off.

FRINGE
Knot a 14-inch length of yarn in each st along short ends alternating colors: MC, A, MC, B, MC. Trim fringe evenly. ★

New England State Flowers
Connecticut: *Mountain laurel*
Maine: *White pinecone and tassel*
Massachusetts: *Mayflower*
New Hampshire: *Purple lilac*
Rhode Island: *Violet*
Vermont: *Red clover*

Baby's Reversible Ripples

Worked with a double-ended crochet hook, this charming afghan is just right for pleasing both the new mother and precious baby!

Design by Darla Fanton

SKILL LEVEL: Beginner

SIZE: 34 x 41 inches

MATERIALS
- Coats & Clark Red Heart Super Saver worsted weight yarn: 5 oz light periwinkle #347, 4 oz light raspberry #774
- Coats & Clark Red Heart Fiesta worsted weight yarn: 9 oz baby white #6301
- Susan Bates size K/10½ double-ended 14-inch crochet hook or size needed to obtain gauge
- Knitting needle protector

GAUGE
4 rows = 1 inch; 4 sts = 1 inch
Check gauge to save time.

PATTERN NOTES
Weave in loose ends as work progresses.

If you have difficulty keeping all of the sts on the hook, cap the unused end of hook with either a knitting needle protector or a clean wine cork.

To pick up a lp in horizontal st, insert hook under top lp only of indicated horizontal st, yo and draw through.

Carry unused color along side edge of afghan; before picking up lps with baby white yarn, draw raspberry and light periwinkle yarn to front and place in front of white lp left on hook, then proceed to draw up lps.

AFGHAN
Row 1: With light periwinkle, ch 198, working from right to left, insert hook in 2nd ch from hook, yo and draw through forming a lp on hook, [keeping all lps on hook, insert hook in next ch, yo and draw through forming a lp on hook] rep across length of foundation ch; slide all sts to opposite end of hook, turn. (198 lps on hook)

Row 2: Place baby white on hook with a sl knot, working from left to right, draw through first lp on hook, [yo, draw through 2 lps on hook (1 lp of each color)] rep across until 1 lp of baby white remains on hook, do not turn.

Row 3: With baby white and working right to left, ch 1, [sk next horizontal st, draw up a lp in next horizontal st] twice, sk next horizontal st, *[yo, draw up a lp in next horizontal st] 6 times, [sk next horizontal st, draw up a lp in next horizontal st] 6 times, rep from * across, ending [sk next horizontal st, draw up a lp in next horizontal st] 3 times; slide all sts to opposite end of hook, turn. (198 lps on hook)

Row 4: Place light raspberry on hook with sl knot, working from left to right, draw through first lp on hook, [yo, draw through 2 lps on hook (1 lp of each color)] rep across until 1 lp of light raspberry remains on hook, do not turn.

Row 5: With light raspberry, rep Row 3.

Row 6: Pick up baby white and working from left to right, yo and draw through first lp, [yo and draw through 2 lps on hook (1 lp of each color)] rep across until 1 lp of baby white remains on hook, do not turn.

Row 7: Rep Row 3.

Row 8: With light periwinkle, rep Row 6.

Row 9: With light periwinkle, rep Row 3.

Row 10: Rep Row 6.

Row 11: Rep Row 3.

Row 12: With light raspberry, rep Row 6.

Rows 13–152: Rep Rows 5–12, ending last rep with Row 8.

Row 153: With light periwinkle and working right to left, insert hook in first horizontal st, yo and draw through st, yo and draw through both lps on hook, [insert hook in next horizontal st, yo, draw through st, yo and draw through both lps on hook] rep across, fasten off. ★

Spring Bouquets

Capture the simple beauty of spring's first blooms with this enchanting afghan! Dainty flower appliqués add dimension and charm!

Design by Carol Alexander

SKILL LEVEL: Beginner

SIZE: 49 x 64 inches

MATERIALS
- Coats & Clark Red Heart Super Saver worsted weight yarn (8 oz per skein): 6 skeins soft white #316, 2 skeins light periwinkle #347, 1 skein each light plum #531, light raspberry #774, cornmeal #320 and paddy green #368
- Size H/8 crochet hook or size needed to obtain gauge
- Yarn needle

GAUGE
Completed square = 7½ inches; 6 sts of square = 2 inches; 5 rows = 2 inches; flower = 2½ inches in diameter

Check gauge to save time.

PATTERN NOTES
Weave in loose ends as work progresses.

Sl st to join each rnd in top of beg st.

Ch 3 counts as first dc throughout.

PATTERN STITCHES
Dtr cl: [Yo hook 3 times, insert hook in indicated st, yo, draw up a lp, {yo, draw through 2 lps on hook} 3 times] twice, yo, draw through all 3 lps on hook.

Long dc: Yo hook, insert hook into center of sc of Rnd 1 of edging directly below, draw up a lp level with working rnd, [yo, draw through 2 lps on hook] twice.

P: Ch 2, sl st in 2nd ch from hook.

AFGHAN SQUARE
(Make 48)

Row 1 (WS): With soft white, ch 19 loosely, dc in 4th ch from hook, sc in next ch, [dc in next ch, sc in next ch] 7 times, turn. (17 sts)

Row 2 (RS): Ch 3, sc in next dc, [dc in next sc, sc in next dc] 6 times, dc in next sc, sk next dc, dc in turning ch, turn. (16 sts)

Row 3: Ch 3, [sc in next dc, dc in next sc] 7 times, sc in turning ch, turn. (16 sts)

Rows 4–14: Rep Row 3.

Note: Square at this point should measure 5¼ inches square.

EDGING
Rnd 1 (RS): Ch 1, [3 sc in corner st, work 14 sc evenly sp across edge] rep around, join in beg sc. (68 sc)

Rnd 2 (RS): Attach light periwinkle in any center corner sc, ch 2 (counts as first hdc throughout), 2 hdc in same st as beg ch-2, *hdc in each sc across to center corner sc **, 3 hdc in center corner sc, rep from * around, ending last rep at **, join in top of beg ch-2, fasten off.

Rnd 3 (RS): Attach soft white in any center corner hdc, ch 3, [dc, ch 2, 2 dc] in same st as beg ch-3, *dc in next hdc, long dc in next st of Rnd 1 of edging, [dc in each of next 2 hdc, long dc in next sc of Rnd 1 of edging] 5 times, dc in next hdc **, [2 dc, ch 2, 2 dc] in next center corner hdc, rep from * around, ending last rep at **, join in top of beg ch-3, fasten off.

ASSEMBLY
With WS of squares facing, working through both lps of each square, sew squares tog 6 x 8.

FLOWER BOUQUETS
Flower
(Make 35 each light raspberry, light periwinkle, cornmeal & light plum)

Leaving a slight length at beg, ch 5, sl st to join in beg ch to form a ring, working over beg rem length and into ring, [ch 3, 3 tr, ch 3, sl st] 5 times in ring, fasten off. (5 petals)

With WS facing, pull rem length at beg to close opening, weave though sts and secure to keep center opening closed. Smooth flower petals and arrange evenly.

With a length of cornmeal, make a large French knot at center of flower.

Leaf
Attach paddy green on WS of flower between any 2 petals, [ch 4, dtr cl, p, ch 4, sl st] in same sp, fasten off.

For each bouquet, using photo as a guide, sew 1 flower of each color to afghan at each point where corners of 4 squares are joined, arranging flowers in a cluster, slightly overlapping with leaves evenly positioned as shown. Alternate position of flower colors in bouquets.

BORDER
Rnd 1 (RS): Attach soft white in any corner ch-2 sp, ch 3, [dc, ch 2, 2 dc] in same ch-2 sp as beg ch-3, *dc evenly sp across to next corner ch-2 sp **, [2 dc, ch 2, 2 dc] in next corner ch-2 sp, rep from * around, ending last rep at **, join in top of beg ch-3.

Rnd 2: Sl st into corner ch-2 sp, ch 3, [dc, ch 2, 2 dc] in corner ch-2 sp, dc in each dc around, working [2 dc, ch 2, 2 dc] in each corner ch-2 sp, sl st to join in top of beg ch-3, fasten off.

Note: On the following rnd, adjust

Continued on page 26

Christmas Home

Warm shades of red, spruce and cream create a lovely, traditional Christmas look in this pretty afghan. Puff stitches worked into a diamond pattern add extra texture!

Design by Eleanor Albano-Miles

SKILL LEVEL: Intermediate

SIZE: 40 x 60 inches

MATERIALS

- Coats & Clark Red Heart Soft worsted weight yarn: 25 oz dark blush #7744 (A) and 16 oz hollyberry #7946 (B)
- Size J/10 crochet hook or size needed to obtain gauge
- Tapestry needle

GAUGE

3 sc = 1 inch; 4 sc rows = 1 inch

Check gauge to save time.

PATTERN NOTES

Weave in loose ends as work progresses.

Sl st to join each rnd in top of beg st.

PATTERN STITCH

Puff st: [Yo hook, insert hook in indicated st, yo, draw up a lp, yo, draw through 2 lps on hook] 3 times in same st, yo, draw through all 4 lps on hook, ch 1 to lock.

PANEL

(Make 5)

Row 1: With A, ch 14, sc in 2nd ch from hook, sc in each rem ch across, turn. (13 sc)

Row 2: Ch 1, sc in each st across, turn.

Row 3: Ch 1, sc in each of next 6 sts, puff st in next st, sc in each of next 6 sts, turn.

Row 4: Rep Row 2.

Row 5: Ch 1, sc in each of next 5 sts, puff st in next st, sc in next st, puff st in next st, sc in each of next 5 sts, turn.

Row 6: Rep Row 2.

Row 7: Ch 1, sc in each of next 4 sts, puff st in next st, sc in each of next 3 sts, puff st in next st, sc in each of next 4 sts, turn.

Row 8: Rep Row 2.

Row 9: Ch 1, sc in each of next 3 sts, puff st in next st, sc in each of next 5 sts, puff st in next st, sc in each of next 3 sts, turn.

Row 10: Rep Row 2.

Row 11: Ch 1, sc in each of next 2 sts, puff st in next st, sc in each of next 7 sts, puff st in next st, sc in each of next 2 sts, turn.

Row 12: Rep Row 2.

Rows 13–20: Rep Rows 11 and 12.

Row 21: Rep Row 9.

Row 22: Rep Row 2.

Row 23: Rep Row 7.

Row 24: Rep Row 2.

Row 25: Rep Row 5.

Row 26: Rep Row 2.

Row 27: Rep Row 3.

Row 28: Rep Row 2.

[Rep Rows 3–28] 7 times.

Rep Row 2, fasten off.

BORDER

Rnd 1 (RS): Attach B with sl st in corner st, ch 1, [{sc, ch 2, sc} in corner st, sc evenly sp across edge] rep around, join in beg sc, turn.

Rnd 2: Ch 3, dc in each st around entire outer edge, working [dc, ch 2, dc] in each corner ch-2 sp, join in top of beg ch-3, fasten off, turn.

Rnd 3: Ch 1, sc in each sc around, working [sc, ch 2, sc] in each corner ch-2 sp, join in beg sc, fasten off.

Rnd 4 (RS): Attach A with sl st in corner ch-2 sp, ch 1, *[sc, ch 2, sc] in corner ch-2 sp, sc in each of next 2 sts, [fpdc around dc of Rnd 2 directly below, sk st directly behind post st, sc in next st] rep across edge, ending with 2 sc before corner ch-2 sp, rep from * around, join in beg sc, turn.

Rnd 5: Rep Rnd 3.

Rnd 6 (RS): Attach B in corner ch-2 sp, ch 1, [{sc, ch 2, sc} in corner ch-2 sp, sc in each st across edge] rep around, join in beg sc.

Rnd 7: Rep Rnd 3, fasten off.

ASSEMBLY

With RS tog and working through back lps only, whipstitch panels tog. ★

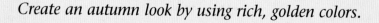

Create an autumn look by using rich, golden colors.

Tasseled Motifs

Each hexagon motif is richly textured with bobbles and long
stitches in this Aran-style afghan. Generous tassels add the finishing touch!

Design by Angela Tate

SKILL LEVEL: Intermediate

SIZE: 52 x 68 inches, excluding tassels

MATERIALS

- Coats & Clark Red Heart Super Saver worsted weight yarn: 64 oz Aran #313
- Size J/10 crochet hook or size needed to obtain gauge
- Tapestry needle

GAUGE

9 dc or Rnd 1 of motif = 3 inches; motif = 8 inches in diameter; 9 inches diagonally

Check gauge to save time.

PATTERN NOTES

Weave in loose ends as work progresses.

Join rnds with a sl st unless otherwise stated.

Ch 3 at beg of a row or rnd counts as first dc throughout.

PATTERN STITCH

Popcorn (pc): 5 dc in indicated st, draw up a lp, remove hook, insert hook in first dc of 5-dc group, pick up dropped lp, draw through st on hook, ch 1 to lock.

MOTIF
(Make 50)

Rnd 1: Ch 12, sl st to join to form a ring, ch 3, 23 dc in ring, join in top of beg ch-3. (24 dc)

Rnd 2: Ch 3, dc in each of next 2 dc, *[2 dc, ch 3, 2 dc] in next dc **, dc in each of next 3 dc, rep from * around, ending last rep at **, join in top of beg ch-3.

Rnd 3: Ch 3, [fpdc around next dc, bpdc around next dc] twice, 5 sc in next ch-3 sp, *[bpdc around next dc, fpdc around next dc] 3 times, bpdc around next dc, 5 sc in next ch-3 sp, rep from * 4 times, bpdc around next dc, fpdc around next dc, join in 3rd ch of beg ch-3.

Rnd 4: Ch 3, [fpdc around next st, bpdc around next st] twice, sc in each of next 2 sc, pc in next sc, sc in each of next 2 sc, *[bpdc around next st, fpdc around next st] 3 times, bpdc around next st, sc in each of next 2 sc, pc in next sc, sc in each of next 2 sc, rep from * 4 times, bpdc around next st, fpdc around next st, join in 3rd ch of beg ch-3.

Rnd 5: Ch 3, [fpdc around next st, bpdc around next st] twice, sc in each of next 2 sc, 3 sc in pc, sc in each of next 2 sc, *[bpdc around next st, fpdc around next st] 3 times, bpdc around next st, sc in each of next 2 sc, 3 sc in pc, sc in each of next 2 sc, rep from * 4 times, bpdc around next st, fpdc around next st, join in 3rd ch of beg ch-3.

Rnd 6: Ch 3, dc in each st around, working 3 dc in 4th sc of 7-sc group, join in 3rd ch of beg ch-3, fasten off.

HALF MOTIF
(Make 8)

Row 1: Ch 10, 2 dc in 4th ch from hook, 3 dc in each rem ch across, turn. (21 dc)

Row 2 (RS): Ch 3, dc in each of next 7 dc, *[2 dc, ch 3, 2 dc] in next dc, dc in each of next 3 dc,

rep from *, dc in each of next 5 dc, turn.

Row 3: Ch 3, [fpdc around next dc, bpdc around next dc] 4 times, fpdc around next dc, 5 dc in next ch-3 sp, [fpdc around next dc, bpdc around next dc] 3 times, fpdc around next dc, 5 sc in next ch-3 sp, [fpdc around next dc, bpdc around next dc] 5 times, turn.

Row 4: Ch 3, [bpdc around next st, fpdc around next st] 4 times, bpdc around next st, *sc in each of next 2 sc, pc in next sc, sc in each of next 2 sc, [bpdc around next st, fpdc around next st] 3 times, bpdc around next st, rep from *, fpdc around next st, bpdc around next st, fpdc around next st, turn.

Row 5: Ch 3, [fpdc around next st, bpdc around next st] 4 times, fpdc around next st, *sc in each of next 2 sc, 3 sc in pc, sc in each of next 2 sc, [fpdc around next st, bpdc around next st] 3 times, fpdc around next st, rep from *, bpdc around next st, fpdc around next st, bpdc around next st, turn.

Row 6: Ch 3, dc in each st across, working 3 dc in 4th sc of 7-sc group, fasten off.

JOINING

With RS facing, working in back lps only, use tapestry needle and yarn to whipstitch motifs tog as follows: Sew 5 strips of 6 motifs each and 4 strips of 5 motifs each. Sew half motifs onto each end of each 5-motif strip. Sew strips into 9 rows of alternating 5- and 6-motif strips, beg and ending with a 6-motif strip.

BORDER

Rnd 1 (RS): Attach yarn with a sl st at free point of any hexagon on end of afghan, ch 1, sc evenly sp around, working [hdc, 2 dc, tr, 2 dc, hdc] across center of each half motif to fill in, join in beg sc.

Rnd 2: Ch 1, reverse sc in each st around, join in beg sc, fasten off.

TASSELS
(Make 12)

Cut 12 (16-inch) strands of yarn. Holding all 12 tog, attach with a Lark's Head Knot to WS of afghan at free point of any end hexagon. Rep in each free point across both ends of afghan. Trim ends of tassels evenly. ★

All-American Plaid
Continued from page 12

vertical stripes, work the center stripe in cornmeal and the 2 outside stripes in gold.

EDGING

Rnd 1: With standard J hook, sl st to join soft navy in any corner, ch 1, 2 hdc in same st, hdc evenly sp around entire outer edge, working 3 hdc in each corner st, sl st to join in beg ch-1.

Rnds 2 & 3: Ch 1, hdc in each st around, working 3 hdc in center corner hdc, sl st to join in beg ch-1.

At the end of Rnd 3, fasten off. ★

American Pride
Continued from page 8

skipper blue and royal blue. With RS facing, sew squares tog.

BORDER

Rnd 1 (RS): With crochet hook size H, draw up a lp of soft navy in first ch-2 sp to the left of either corner on long side edge, ch 1, sc in same sp, [ch 2, sk next 2 sc, sc in next ch-1 sp] 4 times, *ch 2, sk next 2 sc, sc in next corner ch-3 sp, ch 1, sk joining seam, sc in next corner ch-3 sp, [ch 2, sk next 2 sc, sc in next ch-1 sp] 5 times, rep from * around, working corners with ch 2, sk next 2 sc, [sc, ch 3, sc] in corner ch-3 sp, [ch 2, sk next 2 sc, sc in next ch-1 sp] 5 times, ending with join last ch-2 sp with beg sc, turn.

Rnd 2 (WS): Ch 1, skipping over sc sts and working in ch-2 sps, ch-1 sps and corner ch-3 sps, work 2 sc in next sp, working corner pattern ch 1, [sc, ch 3, sc] in corner ch-3 sp, *[ch 1, 2 sc in next ch-2 sp] 6 times, ch 1, sc in next ch-1 sp, rep from * around, working corner pattern in rem 3 corners, join last ch-2 sp in beg sc, turn.

Rnd 3 (RS): Working in ch-1 sps and corner ch-3 sps only, beg shell in next ch-1 sp, sc in next ch-1 sp, *shell in next ch-1 sp, sc

in next ch-1 sp, rep from * around, working in each corner [dc, ch 3, 3 dc] in each corner ch-3 sp, sc in next ch-1 sp, join in top of beg ch-3, sl st into ch-2 sp.

Rnd 4 (RS): With hook size G, ch 3, sl st in same ch sp, skipping over other sts and working in specified sts only, ch 2, sl st in next sc, *ch 2, [sl st, ch 3, sl st] in next ch-2 sp, ch 2, sl st in next sc, rep from * around, working at each corner, ch 2, sk 1 dc, sl st in next dc, ch 2, sk 1 dc, [sl st, ch 2, sl st, ch 3, sl st, ch 2, sl st] in corner ch-3 sp, ch 2, sk 1 dc, sl st in next dc, ch 2, sk 1 dc, sl st in next sc, ending with sl st in same st as beg sl st, fasten off.

With WS facing, block afghan. ★

Spring Bouquets
Continued from page 20

spacing of sts as needed to accommodate st sequence, but maintain consistency between opposite sides.

Rnd 3: Attach light periwinkle in any corner ch-2 sp, ch 4 (counts as first tr), 5 tr in same ch-2 sp, *sk next dc, sc in next dc, sk next dc, [4 tr in next dc, sk next dc, sc in next dc, sk next dc] rep across to corner ch-2 sp **, 6 tr in next ch-2 sp, rep from * around, ending last rep at **, join in top of beg ch-4, fasten off. ★

Painted Daisies

Continued from page 14

inside corners as indicated on Afghan Motif Placement diagram , join in beg sc.

Rnd 3: Sl st into ch sp, ch 4 (counts as first dc, ch 1), dc in same sp, ch 1, [{dc, ch 1} twice in next sp] 19 times, *†[dc, ch 1] 4 times in next sp, [{dc, ch 1} twice in next sp] 3 times, dc in next sp, dc between next 2 sc, dc in next sp, ch 1, [{dc, ch 1} twice in next sp] 8 times †, rep from † to †, [dc, ch 1] 4 times in next sp, [{dc, ch 1} twice in next sp] 20 times, [dc, ch 1] 4 times in next sp, [{dc, ch 1} twice in next sp] 60 times, [dc, ch 1] 4 times in next sp , [{dc, ch 1} twice in next sp] 20 times, rep from * to *, join in 3rd ch of beg ch-4.

Rnd 4: Sl st into ch-1 sp, ch 1, sc in same ch-1 sp, [ch 3, sc in next sp] rep around with the following exception: do not ch 3 on inside corners as indicated on Afghan Motif Placement diagram, ending with dc in beg sc.

Rnd 5: Ch 1, sc in same sp as beg ch-1, ch 3, dc in 3rd ch from hook, sc in next sp, [sc in next sp, ch 3, dc in 3rd ch from hook, sc in next sp] rep around, join in beg sc, fasten off.

Pillow

Following afghan pattern, make 6 each of Triangles 1 and 2. Following Pillow Motif Placement diagram for placement, join 6 motifs each for pillow front and back following the afghan joining instructions.

FRONT BORDER

Rnd 1: Working around pillow front only, attach F in any corner with *sc in joining st, [ch 3, sc in next sp] 10 times, ch 3, rep from * around, join in beg sc.

Rnd 2: Sl st into ch sp, ch 1, sc in same ch sp, ch 3, [sc in next ch sp, ch 3] rep around, join in beg sc.

Rnd 3: Sl st into ch sp, ch 4 (counts as first dc, ch 1), dc in same sp, ch 1, [{dc, ch 1} twice in next ch sp] 9 times, [dc, ch 1] 4 times in next ch sp, *[{dc, ch 1} twice in next sp] 10 times, [dc, ch 1] 4 times in next sp, rep from * around, join in 3rd ch of beg ch-4.

Rnd 4: Sl st into ch-1 sp, ch 1, sc in same ch-1 sp, [ch 3, sc in next ch sp] rep around, ending with dc in beg sc.

Rnd 5: Ch 1, sc in same ch sp as beg ch-1, ch 3, dc in 3rd ch from hook, sc in next ch sp, [sc in next ch sp, ch 3, dc in 3rd ch from hook, sc in next sp] rep around, join in beg sc, fasten off.

FINISHING

With white material, make a 12-inch round pillow and stuff with fiberfill or use a 12-inch pillow form.

With WS of pillow facing and matching joining rnds, sew around, inserting pillow before closing. ★

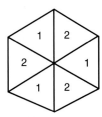

Pillow Motif Placement

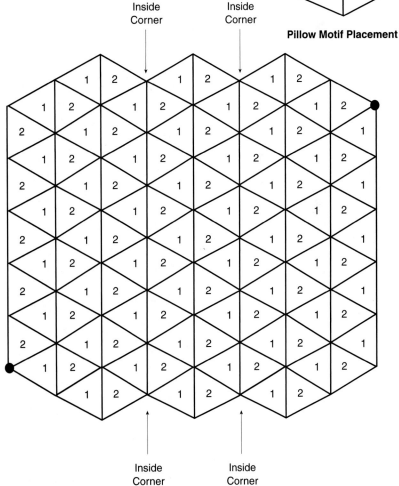

Afghan Motif Placement

Eastern Style

The Eastern region of the country is recognized around the world for its style, sophistication and power. Capture the glamour of the East Coast with this collection of afghans designed for the new millennium!

Stained Glass Motifs

A beautiful, jewel-toned variegated yarn gives each motif in the lovely afghan a look of elegant stained glass! This afghan is a perfect crochet-on-the-go project.

Design by Tammy Hildebrand

SKILL LEVEL: Intermediate

SIZE: 40 x 61 inches

MATERIALS
- Coats & Clark Red Heart Super Saver worsted weight yarn: 17 oz gemstone #959 (MC), 16 oz soft white #316 (CC)
- Size I/9 crochet hook or size needed to obtain gauge
- Tapestry needle

GAUGE
Motif = 4 inches corner to corner; 4 dc = 1 inch
Check gauge to save time.

PATTERN NOTES
Weave in loose ends as work progresses.

Sl st to join each rnd in top of beg st.

Make a total of 91 motifs. Motifs are joined tog in 7 rows of 13 motifs as work progresses.

PATTERN STITCHES
Cross st: Sk next st, dc in next st, working over dc just made, dc in skipped st.

Large cross st: Sk next 3 sts on working motifs, sk next 2 sts on next motif, tr in next st, working over tr just made, tr in first skipped st on previous motif.

Strip joining: Sc in indicated st or sp, ch 1, drop lp from hook, insert hook in center ch of corresponding ch-3 sp on previous strip, pick up dropped lp and draw through, ch 1, sc in same st or sp on working strip.

AFGHAN STRIP
(Make 7)

First motif
Rnd 1 (RS): With MC, ch 3, sl st to join to form a ring, ch 3 (counts as first dc throughout), 2 dc in ring, ch 2, [3 dc in ring, ch 2] 3 times, join in top of beg ch-3, fasten off. (12 dc)

Rnd 2 (RS): Working in back lps of each st for this rnd only, attach CC with sl st in first ch of any corner, ch 3, dc in same ch, ch 2, 2 dc in next ch, dc in each of next 3 sts, [2 dc in next ch, ch 2, 2 dc in next ch, dc in each of next 3 sts] 3 times, sl st to join in top of beg ch, fasten off. (28 dc)

Rnd 3 (RS): Working in back lps of each st for this rnd only, attach MC with sc in first ch of any corner, ch 1, sc in next ch, sc in each of next 7 sts, [sc in next ch, ch 1, sc in next ch, sc in each of next 7 sts] 3 times, sl st to join in beg sc, fasten off. (36 sc)

Second–13th motifs
Rnds 1 & 2: Rep Rnds 1 and 2 of first motif.

Rnd 3 (RS): Working in back lps of each st for this rnd only, attach MC with sc in first ch of any corner, sl st in corresponding ch-1 sp on previous motif, sc in next ch

Continued on page 46

Cheerful Cherries

Lovely to look at and smell in springtime, and filled with juicy cherries in summer, cherry trees are an all-American favorite! Capture the cheeriness of cherries with this unique afghan!

Design by Martha Brooks Stein

PATTERN NOTES
Weave in loose ends as work progresses.

Sl st to join each rnd in top of beg st.

Ch 2 counts as first dc throughout.

SOLID GRANNY SQUARE
Note: Make 190 white, 81 grass green and 35 cherry red.

Rnd 1 (RS): Ch 4, sl st to join to form a ring, ch 2, 2 dc in ring, ch 2, [3 dc in ring, ch 2] 3 times, join in top of beg ch-2. (12 dc; 4 ch-2 sps)

Rnd 2: Ch 2, 2 dc in corner ch-2 sp, ch 1, [{3 dc, ch 2, 3 dc} in next corner ch-2 sp, ch 1] 3 times, 3 dc in same corner ch-2 sp as beg dc sts, ch 2, sl st to join in top of beg ch-2, leaving an 8-inch length of yarn, fasten off.

TWO-COLOR GRANNY SQUARES
Note: Make 34 grass green and white squares and 28 cherry red and white squares.

Rnd 1 (RS): With white, ch 4, sl st to join to form a ring, ch 3, sl st in 2nd ch from hook, holding lp made to right of chs, work [2 dc, ch 2, 3 dc] in ring, leaving a 3-inch tail, fasten off; leaving a 3-inch tail at beg, pick up darker color with sl st, ch 1, [3 dc, ch 2, 3 dc] in ring, sl st to join in lp of beg ch-3, fasten off. Tie ends of first color change in square knot.

Rnd 2 (RS): In last corner that was joined, pick up white, attach with a sl st, ch 3, sl st in 2nd ch from hook, 2 dc in same corner sp, ch 1, [3 dc, ch 2, 3 dc] in next corner ch-2 sp, ch 1, 3 dc in next corner ch-2 sp, leaving a 3-inch tail, fasten off; pick up darker color with sl st, ch 1, 3 dc in same corner sp, ch 1, [3 dc, ch 2, 3 dc] in next corner ch-2 sp, ch 1, 3 dc in same corner sp as beg sts, ch 1, join with sl st in side of beg ch-3, leaving an 8-inch length of yarn, fasten off.

Tie ends of first color change tog.

ASSEMBLY
Using diagram as a guide, sew squares tog. For ease in sewing tog, divide diagram into sections, sew those squares tog and rep until completed, and then sew sections tog. Cut a length of grass green 6 times the length of stem, chain-stitch stems as indicated on diagram.

BORDER
Rnd 1 (RS): Working in back lps for this rnd only, attach cherry red with sl st in 2nd ch of any corner, ch 1, sc in same st, *[sc in each of next 3 dc, sc in next ch sp, sc in each of next 3 dc, sc in next ch sp, sk joining sts, sc in next ch sp of next square] rep across to corner ch-2 sp, sc in first ch of corner, ch 2, sc in 2nd ch of corner, rep from * around, ending with hdc in beg sc to position hook in proper position to beg following rnd.

Rnd 2: Ch 2, dc in corner sp, sk next sc, dc in next sc, *[ch 1, sk next sc, dc in each of next 3 sc] rep across to next corner, ending with ch 1, sk next sc, dc in next sc, [2 dc, ch 2, 2 dc] in corner ch-2 sp, dc in next sc, rep from * around, ending with 2 dc in same sp as beg sts, hdc in top of beg ch-2.

Rnd 3: Ch 2, 2 dc in same corner sp, *[ch 1, 3 dc in next ch-1 sp]

Continued on page 46

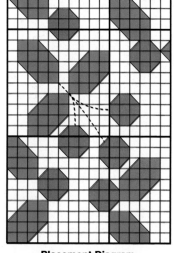

Placement Diagram

City Blocks

This gorgeous afghan has it all—high class, tradition and fabulous color! Small and large granny squares are joined together to make it uniquely stylish!

Design by Carolyn Pfeifer

SKILL LEVEL: Intermediate

SIZE: 51 x 61 inches

MATERIALS
- Coats & Clark Red Heart Super Saver worsted weight yarn: 40 oz heather gray #400, 10 oz black #312, 10 oz light gray #341, 8 oz cherry red #319
- Size I/9 crochet hook or size needed to obtain gauge
- Tapestry needle

GAUGE
Small granny square = 2½ inches; large granny square = 5 inches
Check gauge to save time.

PATTERN NOTES
Weave in loose ends as work progresses.

Sl st to join each rnd in top of beg st.

Complete afghan is made of 30 quilt blocks.

Each quilt block is made of 1 large granny square, 4 black and cherry red small granny squares and 8 heather gray small granny squares.

LARGE GRANNY SQUARE
(Make 30)
Rnd 1 (RS): With cherry red, ch 5, sl st to join to form a ring, ch 3 (counts as first dc throughout), work 19 dc in ring, join in top of beg ch-3, fasten off. (20 dc)

Rnd 2 (RS): Attach light gray in any dc, ch 1, beg in same st as beg ch-1, [sc in each of next 4 dc, ch 4, sk 1 dc] 4 times, join in beg sc. (16 sc)

Rnd 3: Ch 1, [sc in each of next 4 sc, 7 sc in next ch-4 sp] 4 times, join in beg sc. (44 sc)

Rnd 4: Ch 3, dc in each of next 6 sc, *[dc, ch 2, dc] in next sc at corner center **, dc in each of next 10 sc, rep from * around, ending last rep at **, dc in each of next 3 sc, join in top of beg ch-3.

Rnd 5: Ch 1, sc in each of next 8 sc, *7 sc in ch-2 corner sp, sc in each of next 12 dc **, rep from * around, ending last rep at **, sc in each of next 4 dc, join in beg sc, fasten off.

SMALL TWO-COLOR GRANNY SQUARE
(Make 120)

Rnd 1 (RS): With cherry red, ch 4, 15 dc in first ch, join in top of beg ch-4, fasten off. (16 dc)

Rnd 2: Attach black in any dc, ch 1, beg in same st, [sc in each of next 3 dc, ch 3, sk 1 dc] rep around, join in beg sc. (12 sc)

Rnd 3: Ch 1, beg in same sc, [sc in each of next 3 sc, 7 sc in corner ch-3 sp] rep around, join in beg sc, fasten off.

SMALL SOLID GRANNY SQUARE
(Make 240)

Rnds 1–3: With heather gray, rep Rnds 1–3 of small two-color granny square.

ASSEMBLY
Using diagram as a guide, working in back lps only and using corresponding yarn color, sew squares tog as indicated to form 30 quilt blocks. Sew quilt blocks tog 5 x 6 blocks.

Continued on page 47

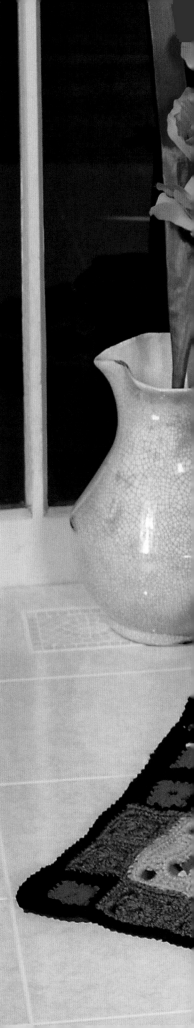

Diagonal Tiles

Glowing pastel blocks cascade across this elegant afghan.
Using a special variety of afghan stitch, the afghan is endlessly
fascinating to watch develop, yet surprisingly simple to create.

Design by Diane Poellot

SKILL LEVEL: Intermediate

SIZE: 40 x 56 inches

MATERIALS

- Coats & Clark Red Heart TLC 3-ply worsted weight yarn: 18 oz natural #5017, 13 oz each spruce #5662, butterscotch #5263, peach #5247
- Size I/9 crochet hook or size needed to obtain gauge
- Tapestry needle

GAUGE

Block = 1⅜ inches square
Check gauge to save time.

PATTERN NOTES

Weave in loose ends as work progresses.

Join rnds with a sl st unless otherwise stated.

PATTERN STITCHES

Knit st: Insert hook between next 2 vertical bars under horizontal sts, yo, draw up a lp (see diagrams on page 44).

Return: [Yo, draw through 2 lps on hook] rep until 1 lp remains on hook.

FIRST STRIP

Row 1: With natural, ch 348, draw up a lp in 2nd ch from hook, draw up a lp in each of next 4 chs, sk next ch, draw this lp through previous lp on hook, return.

Row 2: Knit st next 5 sts, draw up a lp in next ch, draw this lp through previous lp on hook, return.

Rows 3–5: Rep Row 2.

Row 6: Inserting hook as knit st, sl st in next 5 sts, sl st in next ch. (first block completed)

Row 7: Draw up a lp in next 5 chs, sk next ch, draw up a lp in next ch, draw this lp through previous lp on hook, return.

Rep Rows 2–7 to end of beg ch, ending with Row 6, fasten off. (29 blocks)

SECOND STRIP

Row 1: Starting in upper right corner of first block made, with peach, working in back lp of Row 6 sl sts and corresponding back lp of Row 5, draw up a lp in next 5 sts, sk sl st, draw up a lp in first st of Row 1 on next block, draw this lp through previous lp on hook, return.

Rows 2–5: Knit st in next 5 sts, draw up a lp in first st on next row on joining block, draw this lp through previous lp on hook, return.

Row 6: Inserting hook as knit st, sl st in next 5 sts, sl st in corner of joined block (same st as last join).

[{Rep Row 2} 5 times, then Row 6 to end that block] rep across. At the end of last block, omit the last sl st in corner of joined block, fasten off. (28 blocks)

THIRD STRIP

Row 1: Attach spruce with sl st in upper right corner of first block in first strip (same place as last strip was joined), ch 6, draw up a lp in 2nd ch from hook and in each ch across, draw up a lp in first st in end of Row 1 of first block of 2nd strip, draw this lp

through previous lp on hook, return.

Rows 2–6: Rep Rows 2–6 of second strip to end.

LAST BLOCK

Row 1: Working across top of last block on 2nd strip, draw up a lp in next 5 sts, yo, draw through 1 lp, return.

Rows 2–5: Knit st in next 5 sts, yo, draw through 1 lp, return.

Row 6: Inserting hook as knit st, sl st in each st across, fasten off.

Rep 2nd and 3rd strips in color sequence of natural, peach, spruce, then butterscotch, ending with natural, until there are 37 strips.

SIDE EDGING

With natural, join with sl st in first foundation ch of last strip made, sl st in each st down side, skipping sl sts between blocks and adding 1 ch at each point. Rep on opposite side. ★

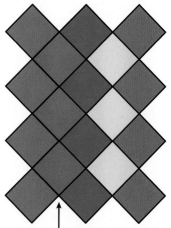

Join here for 2nd and 3rd strips and also for side edging

Assembly Diagram

Pretty Popcorns

Use the popcorn side of this sweet afghan for Baby's playtime. The textured bobbles are sure to please her! For naptime, use the wrong side to give her snuggly warm comfort.

Design by Sue Childress

SKILL LEVEL: Beginner

SIZE: 38 x 43 inches

MATERIALS

- Baby yarn (50 grams per ball): 12 balls pink
- Size F/5 crochet hook or size needed to obtain gauge
- Tapestry needle

GAUGE

5 sc = 1 inch; 5 sc rows = 1 inch
Check gauge to save time.

PATTERN NOTE

Weave in loose ends as work progresses.

PATTERN STITCHES

Popcorn (pc): 5 sc in indicated st, draw up a lp, remove hook, insert hook in first sc of 5-sc group, pick up dropped lp and draw through st on hook.

Shell: [2 dc, ch 2, 2 dc] in indicated st.

AFGHAN

Row 1 (RS): Ch 164, sc in 2nd ch from hook, sc in each rem ch across, turn. (163 sc)

Row 2: Ch 1, sc in each st across, turn.

Rows 3–12: Rep Row 2.

Row 13 (RS): Ch 1, sc in each of next 11 sts, pc in next st, [sc in each of next 19 sts, pc in next st] 7 times, sc in each of next 11 sts, turn.

Row 14 (WS): Ch 1, sc in each st across, turn. (163 sc)

Follow graph until 3 patterns are completed.

EDGING

Rnd 1 (RS): Ch 1, sc evenly sp around entire outer edge, working 3 sc in each corner st, sl st to join in beg sc.

Rnd 2: Ch 3 (counts as first dc throughout), [dc, ch 2, 2 dc] in same sc as beg ch-3, [sk next 3 sc, shell in next sc] rep around entire outer edge, working at each corner [2 dc, ch 2, 2 dc, ch 2, 2 dc] in center sc of each corner, sl st to join in top of beg ch-3.

Rnd 3: Sl st into ch-2 sp, ch 3, 4 dc in same ch-2 sp, [sc between shells, 5 dc in each ch-2 sp of shell] rep around, working at each corner, 5 dc in first ch-2 sp, ch 1, 5 dc in 2nd ch-2 sp, sl st to join in top of beg ch-3, fasten off.

Wet-block afghan. ★

Chart continued on page 45

Bobbles & Squares Delight

Achieve equally stunning, yet totally different results by crocheting this afghan with different colors. For a sunny-skies effect, try a pretty blend of blue, yellow and green yarn!

Design by Eleanor Albano-Miles

SKILL LEVEL: Intermediate

SIZE: 45 x 65 inches

MATERIALS
- Coats & Clark Red Heart Super Saver worsted weight yarn: 30 oz seascape #962 (A) and 32 oz light periwinkle #347 (B)
- Size J/10 crochet hook or size needed to obtain gauge
- Tapestry needle

GAUGE
3 sc sts = 1 inch; 4 sc rows = 1 inch

Check gauge to save time.

PATTERN NOTES
Weave in loose ends as work progresses.

Sl st to join each rnd in beg st.

PATTERN STITCH
Puff st: [Yo hook, insert hook in indicated st, yo, draw up a lp, yo, draw through 2 lps on hook] 3 times in same st, yo, draw through all 4 lps on hook, ch 1 to lock.

For a rich, fall-foliage look, select an autumn-colored variegated and solid.

MOTIF
(Make 24)

Rnd 1 (RS): With A, ch 6, sl st to join to form a ring, ch 3 (counts as first dc throughout), 15 dc in ring, join in top of beg ch-3. (16 dc)

Rnd 2 (RS): Ch 5 (counts as first dc, ch 2 throughout), [dc in next dc, ch 2] rep around, join in 3rd ch of beg ch-5, turn.

Rnd 3 (WS): *[Sc, puff st, sc] in next ch-2 sp, ch 2, rep from * around, join in beg sc.

Rnd 4 (WS): Sl st into ch-2 sp, ch 1, sc in same ch-2 sp, ch 2, [sc in next ch-2 sp, ch 2] rep around, join in beg sc, fasten off, turn.

Rnd 5 (RS): Attach B in any ch-2 sp, ch 1, [3 sc in each of next 3 ch-2 sps, {sc, ch 3, sc} in next ch-2 sp] rep around, join in beg sc, turn.

Rnd 6 (WS): Ch 1, sc in each sc around, working [2 sc, ch 2, 2 sc] in each corner ch-3 sp, join in beg sc, turn.

Rnd 7 (RS): Ch 1, sc in each sc around, working [1 sc, ch 2, 1 sc] in each corner ch-2 sp, join in beg sc, fasten off.

Rnd 8 (WS): Attach A in any corner ch-2 sp, ch 1, *[sc, tr, sc] in corner ch-2 sp, [sc in next st, tr in next st] rep across to corner ch-2 sp, rep from * around, join in beg sc, fasten off.

Rnd 9 (RS): Attach B in corner

Continued on page 47

Argyle & Cables

Here's the perfect gift for that hard-to-please man! This handsome afghan looks knitted, but is really crocheted! A simple cable design sets off panels with a cross-stitch argyle design.

Design by Diane Poellot

SKILL LEVEL: Intermediate

SIZE: 37 x 51 inches

MATERIALS

- Coats & Clark Red heart TLC 3-ply worsted weight yarn: 37 oz natural #5017, 2 oz each spruce #5662 and medium blue #5823

- Size I/9 afghan crochet hook or size needed to obtain gauge

- Tapestry needle

GAUGE

6 knit sts = 1½ inches; 4 rows = 1 inch

Check gauge to save time.

PATTERN NOTE

Weave in loose ends as work progresses.

PATTERN STITCH

Cable twist: Sk next 2 sts, knit in next st, knit in 2nd sk st, knit in first sk st.

AFGHAN

Row 1: With natural, ch 125, draw up a lp in 2nd ch from hook, draw up a lp in each rem ch across, yo, draw through first lp, [yo, draw through 2 lps on hook] rep across until 1 lp remains on hook.

Row 2: Knit in next 3 sts, [purl in next st, knit next 3 sts, purl next st, knit next 9 sts, purl in next st] rep across to last 4 sts, knit last 4 sts, yo, draw through

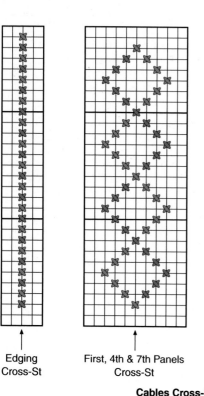

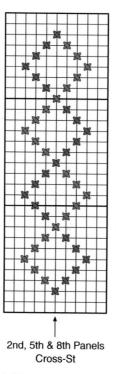

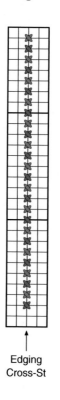

Edging
Cross-St

First, 4th & 7th Panels
Cross-St

2nd, 5th & 8th Panels
Cross-St

Edging
Cross-St

Cables Cross-Stitch Diagram

Raspberry Shells

Picking red and black raspberries is a favorite pastime for those who enjoy making homemade jams and jellies. Stitch this pretty afghan worked in vibrant shades of pink and blue!

Design by Darla Fanton

SKILL LEVEL: Intermediate

SIZE: 44 x 71 inches

MATERIALS

- Coats & Clark Red Heart Super Saver worsted weight yarn: 11 oz raspberry #375 and 9 oz burgundy #376
- Coats & Clark Red Heart Fiesta worsted weight yarn: 20 oz soft navy #6387
- Size K/10½ double-ended crochet hook or size needed to obtain gauge
- Size J/10 crochet hook
- Tapestry needle

GAUGE

1 shell = 1 inch; 4 rows = 1 inch
Check gauge to save time.

PATTERN NOTES

Weave in loose ends as work progresses.

If you have difficulty keeping all of the sts on the hook, cap the unused end of hook with either a knitting needle protector or a clean wine cork.

Carry unused yarn along side edge by holding strands up and to the front before ch 1 on pick up rows. This will lock them in place, making a neater edge.

When working ch 4 on even numbered rows use care not to pull them too tightly, as you will be picking up a lp in each ch on the following row.

AFGHAN

Row 1: With soft navy, ch 197, to pick up a lp, working through back lp only, insert hook in 2nd ch from hook, yo and draw through, [insert hook in back lp of next ch, yo and draw through] rep across foundation ch retaining all lps on hook; slide all sts to opposite end of hook and turn. (197 lps on hook)

Row 2: To work lps off hook, place burgundy on hook with sl knot, working from left to right, draw through first lp, ch 1, draw through 4 lps, [ch 4, draw through next 4 lps] rep across until 1 lp rem on hook; do not turn.

Row 3: With burgundy and working right to left, ch 1, [sk next shell, pick up lp in each of next 4 ch] rep across, ending with sk last shell, pick up lp in last ch; slide all sts to opposite end of hook and turn. (194 lps on hook)

Row 4: Pick up soft navy, yo and draw through 1 lp, ch 5, draw through 4 lps, [ch 4, draw through 4 lps] rep across until 2 lps rem on hook, ch 3, draw through last lp; do not turn.

Row 5: With soft navy, ch 1, pick up lp in each of next 3 ch, [sk shell, pick up lp in each of next 4 ch] rep across, ending with pick up lp in each of last 5 ch; slide all sts to opposite end of hook and turn. (197 lps on hook)

Rows 6 & 7: With raspberry, rep Rows 2 and 3.

Rows 8 & 9: Rep Rows 4 and 5.

Row 10: Pick up burgundy, yo and draw through 1 lp, ch 1, draw through 4 lps, [ch 4, draw through next 4 lps] rep across until 1 lp rem on hook, do not turn.

Rows 11–13: Rep Rows 3–5.

Row 14: With raspberry, rep Row 10.

Rows 15–277: Rep Rows 7–14, ending last rep at the end of a Row 13, do not turn at the end of last rep.

Row 278: Bind off in the following manner; with soft navy, working left to right, yo and draw through 1 lp, ch 1, draw through 4 lps, [ch 3, draw through next 4 lps] rep across, ch 2, transfer remaining lp to size J hook for edging, fasten off burgundy and raspberry.

FIRST SIDE EDGING

Row 1: Turn, working in ends of rows with predominantly soft navy side facing, [work 3 dc in next sp at end of burgundy or raspberry row, ch 1] rep along side edge, ending with ch 2, sl st in end of foundation ch, fasten off.

SECOND SIDE EDGING

Row 1: With predominantly soft navy side facing, attach soft navy with sl st in beg foundation ch, ch 2, [work 3 dc in next sp at end of burgundy or raspberry row, ch 1] rep along edge, ending with ch 2, sl st in beg ch-1 of Row 278, fasten off.

BORDER

Note: Border is designed to ruffle.

Rnd 1: With predominantly soft navy side facing, attach raspberry with sc in any ch-1 sp on a side edge, in same sp work hdc, 3 dc, hdc and sc, [ch 1, {sc, hdc, 3 dc, hdc, sc} in each ch-1 sp, {sc, hdc, 5 dc, hdc, sc} in ch-2 corner sp] rep around, working in sps between soft navy shells on top and bottom edges and ch-1 sps on side edges, sl st to join in beg sc, fasten off. ★

Fields of Corn

With a little imagination, this afghan is reminiscent of perfectly straight rows of golden, tasseled corn ready to be harvested.

Design by Melissa Leapman

SKILL LEVEL: Beginner

SIZE: 46 x 56 inches

MATERIALS
- Elmore-Pisgah's 'Peaches and Cream' cotton yarn (2½ oz per skein): 17 skeins yellow #E10
- Size H/8 afghan crochet hook or size needed to obtain gauge
- Yarn needle

GAUGE
3 dc mesh pattern rows = 1¾ inches; [dc, ch 1] twice and 1 dc = 1 inch

Check gauge to save time.

PATTERN NOTES
Weave in loose ends as work progresses.

PATTERN STITCH
Shell: 5 dc in indicated st.

AFGHAN
Row 1 (RS): Ch 188, dc in 6th ch from hook, ch 1, sk next ch, dc in next ch, [sk next 2 ch, shell in next ch, sk next 2 ch, {dc in next ch, ch 1, sk next ch} twice, dc in next ch] rep across, turn.

Row 2: Ch 4 (counts as first dc, ch 1 throughout), dc in next dc, ch 1, dc in next dc, *sk next 2 dc of shell, shell in next dc of shell, sk next 2 dc of shell, [dc in next dc, ch 1] twice **, dc in next dc, rep from * across, ending last rep at **, sk next ch, dc in next ch of turning ch, turn.

Rep Row 2 until afghan measures 55 inches from beg ending on a WS row.

Row 3 (RS): Ch 4, dc in next dc, ch 1, dc in next dc, *ch 2, sk next 2 dc of shell, sc in next dc, ch 2, sk next 2 dc of shell, [dc in next dc, ch 1] twice **, dc in next dc, rep from * across, ending last rep at **, sk next ch, dc in next ch of turning ch, fasten off.

BORDER
Rnd 1 (RS): Attach yarn in any st, ch 1, sc evenly sp around entire outer edge, working 3 sc in each corner st, sl st to join in beg sc.

Rnds 2 & 3: Ch 1, sc in each sc around, working 3 sc in center sc of each corner, sl st to join in beg sc, fasten off. ★

Midwest State Flowers
Illinois: *Purple Violet*

Indiana: *Peony*

Iowa: *Wild Prairie Rose*

Michigan: *Apple Blossom*

Ohio: *Scarlet Carnation*

Summer Picnic

Pack up a lunch of fried chicken, potato salad and chocolate cake, and take your family on an old-fashioned picnic! This patriotic afghan makes the perfect blanket for your outdoor feast!

Design by Martha Brooks Stein

SKILL LEVEL: Beginner

SIZE: 37 x 51 inches

MATERIALS

- Coats & Clark Red Heart Classic worsted weight yarn: 19 oz white #1, 13½ oz each cherry red #912 and olympic blue #849
- Size I/9 afghan crochet hook or size needed to obtain gauge
- Tapestry needle

GAUGE

Square = 2¾ inches; 5 sc = 1½ inches

Check gauge to save time.

PATTERN NOTES

Weave in loose ends as work progresses.

Sl st to join each rnd unless otherwise indicated.

Make 154 white, 94 cherry red and 104 olympic blue granny square motifs.

AFGHAN MOTIFS

Rnd 1 (RS): Ch 4, sl st to join in first ch to form a ring, ch 2 (counts as first dc throughout), 2 dc in ring, [ch 2, 3 dc in ring] 3 times, hdc in top of beg ch-2 to form last corner sp.

Rnd 2: Ch 2, 2 dc in corner sp, ch 1, [{3 dc, ch 2, 3 dc} in next ch-2 sp, ch 1] 3 times, 3 dc in same corner as beg sts, ch 2, join in top of beg ch-2, leaving an 8-inch length, fasten off.

ASSEMBLY

Working in back lps only, following diagram, sew squares tog.

BORDER

Rnd 1 (RS): Working in back lps for this rnd only, attach olympic blue in upper right corner in 2nd ch of corner ch-2 sp, ch 1, sc in same st, *[sc in each of next 3 dc, sc in ch-1 sp, sc in each of next 3 dc, sc in next ch sp, sk joining, sc in ch sp of next sp] rep across to corner, sc in first ch of corner ch-2 sp, ch 2, sc in 2nd ch of same corner, rep from * around, ending last rep at **, join in beg sc.

Rnd 2 (RS): Ch 2, dc in same corner sp, sk next sc, dc in next sc, *[ch 1, sk next sc, dc in each of next 3 sc] rep across to next corner, ending with ch 1, sk next sc, dc in last sc before corner ch-2 sp, [2 dc, ch 2, 2 dc] in corner ch-2 sp, dc in next sc, rep from * around, adjusting as needed at each corner to end evenly, join in top of beg ch-3, fasten off.

Rnd 3: Attach white with sl st in any ch-2 corner sp, ch 2, 2 dc in same sp, *[ch 1, 3 dc in next ch-1 sp] rep across to next corner ch-2 sp, ch 1, [3 dc, ch 2, 3 dc] in corner ch-2 sp, rep from * around, ending with ch 1, 3 dc in same corner sp as beg sts, ch 2, join in top of beg ch-2, fasten off.

Rnd 4: With cherry red, rep Rnd 4, do not fasten off.

Rnd 5: *[Ch 2, sl st in first dc of next 3-dc group, ch 2, sl st in 3rd dc of same 3-dc group] rep across to corner ch-2 sp, ch 2, sl st in corner ch-2 sp, rep from * around, ending with ch 2, sl st in beg sl st, fasten off. ★

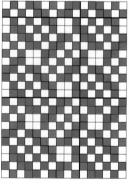

Motif Placement Diagram

COLOR KEY
☐ White
■ Cherry red
■ Olympic blue

Colorful Bricks

Many Amish in the Midwest enjoy quilting bees at which they join their scraps of brightly colored fabric into beautiful quilts for a just-married daughter. Turn your scraps of yarn into this creation and give it to your daughter on her wedding day.

Design by Darla Fanton

SKILL LEVEL: Intermediate

SIZE: 53 x 71 inches

MATERIALS
- Coats & Clark Red Heart Super Saver worsted weight yarn: 19 oz soft navy #387, 10 oz soft white #316, approximately 5 yds each of assorted colors for each brick, approximately 45 yds desired scrap color for final border
- Size K/10 ½ crochet hook or size needed to obtain gauge
- Tapestry needle

GAUGE
15 hdc sts = 5 inches; 14 rows = 5 inches
Check gauge to save time.

PATTERN NOTES
Weave in loose ends as work progresses.

When changing colors, work off last 3 lps of first color with new color, dropping first color to WS of work. Use a separate ball of color for each section. Do not carry yarn across back of work. Fasten off each color when no longer needed.

PANELS
(Make 11)

Row 1: With soft navy, ch 16, hdc in 2nd ch from hook, hdc in each rem ch across, turn. (15 hdc)

Rows 2–27: Ch 1, hdc in each st across, changing colors as needed according to graph, turn.

Rows 28–187: Rep Rows 8–27 of graph.

Rows 188 & 189: Work according to graph.

ASSEMBLY
With tapestry needle and soft navy yarn, sew panels tog.

BORDER
Rnd 1 (RS): Attach soft navy with sl st in any corner, ch 2 (counts as first hdc throughout), [2 hdc, ch 1, 3 hdc] in same st, hdc evenly sp around entire outer edge, working [3 hdc, ch 1, 3 hdc] in each corner, sl st to join in top of beg ch-2.

Rnd 2: Sl st into corner ch-1 sp, [ch 2, 2 hdc, ch 1, 3 hdc] in same ch-1 sp, hdc in each hdc around, working [3 hdc, ch 1, 3 hdc] in each corner ch-1 sp, sl st to join in top of beg ch-2, fasten off.

Rnd 3: Attach desired scrap color in any st, ch 1, sc in same st as beg ch-1, sc in each hdc around, sc in each corner ch-1 sp, sl st to join in beg sc, fasten off. ★

COLOR KEY
- ■ Soft navy
- □ Soft white
- ■ Desired scrap colors
- ▢
- ▢
- ▢
- ■
- ■

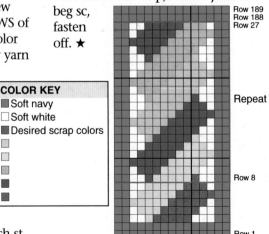

Afghan Graph Panel

Row 189
Row 188
Row 27

Repeat

Row 8

Row 1

Log Cabin Comfort

Remember the labor of the early frontiersmen and women as they settled the Great Plains, building log cabins as their first homes in a free land. Crochet this handsome afghan as a tribute to them.

Design by Kathleen Garen

SKILL LEVEL: Intermediate

SIZE: 47 x 63 inches

MATERIALS
- Worsted weight yarn: 19 oz tan, 8 oz each colonial blue and burgundy
- Coats & Clark Red Heart Super Saver worsted weight yarn: 14 oz painted desert print #303
- Size I/9 afghan crochet hook or size needed to obtain gauge
- Tapestry needle

GAUGE
Square = 14 inches; Rnd 1 of center motif = 9¾ inches; [ch 1, dc in last sp worked and in next ch-1 sp tog] 8 times = 5 inches
Check gauge to save time.

PATTERN NOTES
Weave in loose ends as work progresses.

Sl st to join each rnd in indicated st.

Make 6 squares each burgundy and colonial blue.

PATTERN STITCHES
2-dc cl: [Yo, insert hook in indicated sp, yo, draw up a lp, yo, draw through 2 lps on hook] twice, yo, draw through all 3 lps on hook.

Dc dec over 2 sps: Yo, insert hook in same sp as previous sts were worked, yo, draw up a lp, yo, draw through 2 lps on hook, yo, insert hook in next sp, yo, draw up a lp, yo, draw through 2 lps on hook, yo, draw through all 3 lps on hook.

SQUARES
(Make 12)
Center Motif
(Make 3)

Rnd 1 (RS): With tan, ch 30, hdc in 4th ch from hook, hdc in next ch, [ch 1, sk 1 ch, hdc in next ch] 11 times, hdc in next ch, leaving last 2 chs unworked, ch 1, join with a sl st in last ch.

Rnd 2: In sp created at end of ch, sc, ch 1, dc, *ch 2, 2-dc cl, ch 1, sk the 2 hdc of Rnd 1, dc dec over same and next sp, [ch 1, dc dec over same and next sp] 11 times (ending with last dc of dc dec in end sp), ch 1, 2-dc cl, ch 2, 2-dc cl, ch 1 *, 2-dc cl in same end sp, rep from * to *, join in top of first dc of rnd. (32 ch sps)

Rnd 3: Attach colonial blue (burgundy) with sc in any ch-1 sp on side edge, ch 1, dc in next sp, [ch 1, *dc dec over 2 sps] rep to corner ch-2 sp, ending with last dc of dc dec in corner ch-2 sp, [ch 1, dc, ch 2, dc, ch 1] in corner ch-2 sp, rep from * around, join in top of first dc, fasten off. (40 ch sps)

Joining Center Motifs
Holding 2 center motifs tog, with the back piece slightly higher,

Continued on page 67

Winter Wheat

In the Midwest, many farmers make the most of their ground year-round by planting a crop of wheat that grows during the winter. Stitch this soft afghan to add a touch of homespun, country charm to your house!

Design by Tammy Hildebrand

SKILL LEVEL: Beginner

SIZE: 44 x 63 inches

MATERIALS
- Lion Brand Homespun textured yarn: 33 oz hepplewhite #300 (MC) and 11 oz sierra #318 (CC)
- Size P/16 crochet hook or size needed to obtain gauge
- Tapestry needle

GAUGE
2 sc and 1 shell = 3 inches; 6 rows = 4½ inches

Check gauge to save time.

PATTERN NOTES
Weave in loose ends as work progresses.

Ch 3 counts as first dc throughout.

PATTERN STITCH
Shell: 5 dc in indicated st.

AFGHAN
Row 1 (RS): With MC, ch 92, sc in 2nd ch from hook, sk next 2 ch, shell in next ch, [sk next 2 ch, sc in next ch, sk next 2 ch, shell in next ch] 14 times, sk next 2 ch, sc in last ch, fasten off.

Row 2 (RS): Attach CC with sl st in first sc, ch 3, dc in same st, [sc in center dc of next shell, shell in next sc] 14 times, sc in center dc of next shell, 2 dc in last sc, fasten off.

Row 3 (RS): Attach MC in top of beg ch-3, ch 1, sc in same st as beg ch-1, [shell in next sc, sc in center dc of next shell] 14 times, shell in next sc, sc in last dc, turn.

Row 4 (WS): Ch 3, dc in same st as beg ch-3, [sc in center dc of next shell, shell in next sc] 14 times, sc in center dc of next shell, 2 dc in last sc, turn.

Row 5 (RS): Ch 1, sc in same st as beg ch-1, [shell in next sc, sc in center dc of shell] 14 times, shell in next sc, sc in last dc, fasten off.

[Rep Rows 2–5] 15 times.

[Rep Rows 2 and 3] once. At the end of last rep, fasten off.

FRINGE
With MC, cut 2 lengths of yarn each 14 inches long. Knot 2 strands in each lp along bottom foundation ch and each st along top of last row. Trim ends evenly. ★

Interesting Facts About Wheat

The graham cracker was named after the Rev. Sylvester Graham, who strongly believed in eating whole wheat flour products.

Wheat is grown in 42 U.S. states.

One bushel of wheat contains about one million kernels.

A family of four could live for 10 years off of the bread produced by one acre of wheat.

Golden Harvest Cables

Toward the end of September, the rich fields in the Midwest turn a beautiful shade of gold. Celebrate our country's bounty with this shimmering afghan.

Design by Jo Hanna Dzikowski

SKILL LEVEL: Advanced

SIZE: 37 x 51 inches

MATERIALS
- Worsted weight yarn: 30 oz gold
- Size I/9 crochet hook or size needed to obtain gauge
- 6-inch piece cardboard
- Tapestry needle

GAUGE
3 dc = 1 inch; 7 rows = 4 inches
Check gauge to save time.

PATTERN NOTES
Weave in loose ends as work progresses.

Beg ch 3 counts as first dc throughout.

Use care when following pattern that appropriate sts are utilized.

When working the cable twist, the cable is not always worked over the same 4 sts, which makes the cable pattern waiver.

PATTERN STITCHES
Front post puff stitch (fp puff st): Yo hook, insert hook front to back to front again around the vertical post of next st, yo, draw up a lp, [yo, insert hook from front to back to front again around the same vertical post, yo, draw up a lp] 3 times, yo, draw through all 9 lps on hook, ch 1 to lock.

Puff stitch (puff st): Yo hook, insert hook in next st, yo, draw up a lp, [yo hook insert hook in same st, yo, draw up a lp] 4 times (11 lps on hook), yo, draw through all 11 lps on hook, ch 1 to lock.

Front post dc (fpdc): Yo hook, insert hook front to back to front again around vertical post of next st, yo, draw up a lp, [yo, draw through 2 lps on hook] twice.

Back post dc (bpdc): Yo hook, insert hook back to front to back again around the vertical post of next st, yo, draw up a lp, [yo, draw through 2 lps on hook] twice.

Front post tr (fptr): Yo hook twice, insert hook from front to back to front again around vertical post of next st, yo, draw up a lp, [yo, draw through 2 lps on hook] 3 times.

Back post tr (bptr): Yo hook twice, insert hook from back to front to back again around vertical post of next st, yo, draw up a lp, [yo, draw through 2 lps on hook] 3 times.

Cable twist: Sk next 2 sts, fptr around each of next 2 sts, fptr around 2nd skipped st, fptr around first skipped st.

AFGHAN
Row 1 (WS): Ch 115, dc in 3rd ch from hook, dc in each rem ch across, turn. (113 dc)

Row 2 (RS): Ch 3, dc in next st, *[fpdc around next st, dc in next st] twice, dc in each of next 13 sts, [dc in next st, fpdc around next st] twice **, dc in each of next 6 sts, cable twist over next 4

sts, dc in next st, fp puff st around next st, dc in next st, cable twist over next 4 sts, dc in each of next 6 sts, rep from *, ending last rep at ** dc in each of next 2 sts, turn.

Row 3 (WS): Ch 3, dc in next st, *[bpdc around next st, dc in next st] twice, [dc in next st, bptr around next st, puff st in next st, bptr around next st] 3 times, dc in next st, [dc in next st, bptr around next st] twice **, dc in each of next 6 sts, bptr around each of next 4 sts, dc in each of next 3 sts, bptr around each of next 4 sts, dc in each of next 6 sts, rep from *, ending last rep at **, dc in each of next 2 sts, turn.

Row 4 (RS): Ch 3, dc in next st, *[fpdc around next st, dc in next st] twice, [dc in next st, fptr around st after puff st of previous row, dc in top of puff st, fptr around st before puff st of previous row] 3 times, dc in next st, [dc in next st, fpdc around next st] twice **, dc in next 4 sts, cable twist, dc in next 3 sts, fp puff st around next st, dc in next 3 sts, cable twist, dc in next 4 sts, rep from *, ending last rep at **, dc in each of next 2 dc, turn.

Row 5 (WS): Ch 3, dc in next st, *[bpdc around next st, dc in next st] twice, [dc in next st, bptr around next st, puff st in next st, bptr around next st] 3 times, dc in next st, [dc in next st, bpdc

around next st] twice **, dc in next 4 sts, bptr around next 4 sts, dc in next 7 sts, bptr around next 4 sts, dc in next 4 sts, rep from *, ending last rep at **, dc in each of next 2 sts, turn.

Row 6 (RS): Ch 3, dc in next st, *[fpdc around next st, dc in next st] twice, [dc in next st, fptr around st after puff st of previous row, dc in puff st, fptr around st before puff st of previous row] 3 times, dc in next st, [dc in next st, fpdc around next st] twice **, dc in next 2 sts, cable twist, dc in each of next 5 sts, fp puff st around next st, dc in each of next 5 sts, cable twist, dc in each of next 2 sts, rep from *, ending last rep at **, dc in next 2 sts, turn.

Row 7 (WS): Ch 3, dc in next st, *[bpdc around next st, dc in next st] twice, [dc in next st, bptr around next st, puff st in next st, bptr around next st] 3 times, dc in next st, [dc in next st, bpdc around next st] twice **, dc in next 2 sts, bptr around next 4 sts, dc in next 11 sts, bptr around next 4 sts, dc in each of next 2 sts, rep from *, ending last rep at **, dc in each of next 2 sts, turn.

Row 8 (RS): Ch 3, dc in next st, *[fpdc around next st, dc in next st] twice, [dc in next st, fptr around next st after puff st of previous row, dc in puff st, fptr around st before puff st of previous row] 3 times, dc in next st, [dc in next st, fpdc around next st] twice **, dc in each of next 4 sts, cable twist, dc in next 3 sts, fp puff st around next st, dc in each of next 3 sts, cable twist, dc in each of next 4 sts, rep from *, ending last rep at **, dc in each of next 2 sts, turn.

Row 9 (WS): Ch 3, dc in next st, *[bpdc around next st, dc in next st] twice, [dc in next st, bptr around next st, puff st in next st, bptr around next st] 3 times, dc in next st, [dc in next st, bpdc around next st] twice **, dc in next 4 sts, bptr around next 4 sts, dc in each of next 7 sts, bptr around next 4

sts, dc in each of next 4 sts, rep from *, ending last rep at **, dc in each of next 2 dc, turn.

Row 10 (RS): Ch 3, dc in next st, *[fpdc around next st, dc in next st] twice, [dc in next st, fptr around st after puff st of previous row, dc in puff st, fptr around st before puff st of previous row] 3 times, dc in next st, [dc in next st, fpdc around next st] twice **, dc in next 6 dc, cable twist, dc in next st, fp puff st around next st, dc in next st, cable twist, dc in next 6 dc, rep from *, ending last rep at **, dc in each of next 2 dc, turn.

Rows 11–83: Rep Rows 3–10.

Row 84: Ch 3, dc in each st across, fasten off.

FRINGE
*Wrap yarn 10 times around 6-inch piece of cardboard, cut bottom end of yarn strands. Fold strands in half, insert hook in first st, draw fold through st on hook to form a lp, draw cut ends through lp on hook, pull gently to secure. Sk next 4 sts, rep from * across end of afghan. Rep fringe on opposite end of afghan. Trim ends evenly. ★

Midwest State Songs

Illinois: *Illinois*

Indiana: *On the Banks of the Wabash*

Iowa: *The Song of Iowa*

Kansas: *Home on the Range*

Michigan: *Michigan, My Michigan*

Minnesota: *Hail! Minnesota*

Missouri: *Missouri Waltz*

Nebraska: *Beautiful Nebraska*

North Dakota: *North Dakota Hymn*

Ohio: *Beautiful Ohio*

South Dakota: *Hail, South Dakota*

Wisconsin: *On Wisconsin*

Simple Shells
Continued from page 56

PATTERN NOTE
Weave in loose ends as work progresses.

PATTERN STITCHES
Open shell: [Dc, ch 3, dc] in indicated st.
V-st: [Dc, ch 1, dc] in indicated st.
Shell: [3 dc, ch 1, 3 dc] in indicated st.

AFGHAN
Row 1 (WS): Ch 178, dc in 4th ch from hook, *sk next 2 ch, open shell in next ch, sk next 2 ch **, V-st in next ch, rep from * across, ending last rep at **, 2 dc in last ch, turn.
Row 2 (RS): Ch 1, sc in first dc, shell in next ch-3 sp, [sc in next ch-1 sp, shell in next ch-3 sp] rep across, ending with sc in top of ch-3, turn. (29 shells)
Row 3 (WS): Ch 3, dc in same sc, open shell in next ch-1 sp, [V-st in next sc, open shell in next ch-1 sp] rep across, ending with 2 dc last sc, turn.
Rep Rows 2 and 3 until afghan measures 45 inches, ending with Row 3, fasten off.

BORDER
Rnd 1 (RS): Attach yarn with sl st in upper right corner of afghan, ch 1, working across top edge, work 173 sc evenly sp across, 3 sc in corner st, 215 sc evenly sp across long edge, 3 sc in corner st, 173 sc across opposite side of foundation ch, 3 sc in corner st, 215 sc evenly sp across long edge, 3 sc in corner st, sl st to join in beg sc.
Rnd 2: Ch 1, [sc, ch 3, sc] in same sc as beg ch-1, sk next sc, [{sc, ch 3, sc} in next sc, sk next sc] rep around, sl st to join in beg sc, fasten off. ★

Log Cabin Comfort
Continued from page 60

attach painted desert print in front ch-2 corner sp with sc, ch 1, 2 sc in corner sp of back motif, ch 1, sc again in first front corner, [ch 1, work 2 sc in next back ch-1 sp, ch 1, 2 sc in next front ch-1 sp] rep across to end, 1 sc in back corner, ch 1, 2 sc in front corner, ch 1, 1 sc in same back corner, fasten off.

Join the 3rd center motif to the 2nd center motif in same manner, do not fasten off.

Border
Rnd 1 (RS): Sc around last ch-1, ch 1, dc in corner sp, ch 1, *dc dec over 2 sps, using the joining ch as a sp and working the corners as in center motif, join in top of beg dc, fasten off.

Rnd 2: Attach colonial blue (burgundy) with sc in any ch-1 sp on side edge, rep as for Rnd 3 of center motif, join in top of first dc, fasten off.

Rnd 3: Attach tan with sc in any ch-1 sp on side edge, rep as for Rnd 3 of center motif, join in top of first dc, fasten off.

ASSEMBLY
Squares are joined 3 x 4. All colonial blue squares the center motifs will be positioned vertically and all burgundy squares the center motifs are horizontal. First vertical row of squares is [colonial blue, burgundy] twice, thereafter alternate colors until all 3 rows are completed joining squares in same manner joining center motifs. Then join the 3 strips in same manner as joining center motifs.

TRIM
Rnd 1 (WS): With painted desert print, rep Rnd 1 of border, fasten off.

Rnd 2 (RS): Attach tan, rep Rnd 1 of border.

Rnd 3 (WS): Ch 1, work 2 sc in each ch-1 sp and 4 sc in each corner ch sp around, join in beg sc, fasten off.

Rnd 4 (RS): Attach painted desert print with sl st in any st, ch 1, [sl st in next st, ch 1] rep around, join, fasten off. ★

Southern Hospitality

The Southern states are known for their warm hospitality and slower pace. Southern women are pleased to open their homes to friends and newcomers alike for a piece of pecan pie and a tall glass of lemonade. Take a respite from your busy life—envision yourself on a grand porch swing enjoying a warm summer breeze as you crochet your newest afghan delight.

Sunny Days

*Two different granny square designs are
alternately joined together to make this pretty
afghan. Stitch it in golden yellow with floral color
accents for the look and feel of a bright, sunny day!*

Design by Anne Halliday

SKILL LEVEL: Beginner

SIZE: 55 x 68 inches

MATERIALS

- Coats & Clark Red Heart
  Super Saver worsted weight
  yarn (8 oz per skein): 24 oz
  cornmeal #320 (MC), 8 oz
  white #311 (A), 8 oz light
  raspberry #774 (B), 8 oz
  light sage #631 (C)

- Size I/9 crochet hook or size
  needed to obtain gauge

- Tapestry needle

GAUGE

Square = 6½ inches

Check gauge to save time.

PATTERN NOTES

Weave in loose ends as work
progresses.

Join rnds with a sl st unless otherwise stated.

Rnd 1 establishes RS of squares.

Ch 3 counts as first dc throughout.

PATTERN STITCHES

3-dc cl: [Yo hook, insert hook in
next dc, yo, draw up a lp, yo,
draw through 2 lps on hook] 3
times, yo, draw through all 4 lps
on hook.

Beg 3-dc cl: Ch 2, [yo hook,
insert hook in next dc, yo, draw
up a lp, yo, draw through 2 lps
on hook] twice, yo, draw through
all 3 lps on hook.

Picot (p): Ch 3, yo, insert hook
in 3rd ch from hook, yo, draw up
a lp, yo, draw through 2 lps on

hook, yo, insert hook in same ch,
yo, draw up a lp, yo, draw
through 2 lps on hook, yo, draw
through all 3 lps on hook.

SQUARE A
(Make 32)

Rnd 1 (RS): With A, ch 5, 2 dc
in 5th ch from hook, ch 3, [3 dc,
ch 3] 3 times in same ch, join in
top of beg ch-3, fasten off. (12 dc;
4 ch-3 sps)

Rnd 2: Attach MC in any corner
ch-3 sp, [ch 3, 2 dc, ch 3, 3 dc] in
same sp, ch 1, [{3 dc, ch 3, 3 dc}
in next corner ch-3 sp, ch 1] 3
times, join in top of beg ch-3, fasten off.

Rnd 3: Attach B in any corner
ch-3 sp, [ch 3, 2 dc, ch 3, 3 dc] in
same sp, *ch 1, 3 dc in next ch-1
sp, ch 1 **, [3 dc, ch 3, 3 dc] in
next corner ch-3 sp, rep from *
around, ending last rep at **, join
in top of beg ch-3, fasten off.

Rnd 4: Attach C in any corner
ch-3 sp, [ch 3, 2 dc, ch 3, 3 dc] in
same sp, *ch 1, [3 dc in next ch-1
sp, ch 1] twice **, [3 dc, ch 3, 3 dc]
in next corner ch-3 sp, rep from *
around, ending last rep at **, join
in top of beg ch-3, fasten off.

Rnd 5: Attach MC in any corner
ch-3 sp, [ch 3, 2 dc, ch 3, 3 dc] in
corner same sp, *ch 1, [3 dc in
next ch-1 sp, ch 1] 3 times **, [3
dc, ch 3, 3 dc] in next corner ch-3
sp, rep from * around, ending last
rep at **, join in top of beg ch-3,
fasten off.

SQUARE B
(Make 31)

Rnd 1 (RS): With MC, ch 5, [dc,

times, rep from * across to last ch-4 sp, sc in last ch-4 sp, ch 2, tr in last sc, turn.

Row 13: Ch 1, sc in tr, ch 4, *sc in next ch-4 sp, ch 3, sk next ch-3 sp, shell in next ch-2 sp, ch 2, 3 dc in next ch-3 sp, shell in next ch-2 sp, ch 2, 3 dc in next ch-3 sp, ch 2, shell in next ch-2 sp, ch 3, sk next ch-3 sp, [sc in next ch-4 sp, ch 4] twice, rep from *across to turning ch, sc in 4th ch of turning ch-6, turn.

Rows 14–98: [Rep Rows 2–13] 7 times.

Row 99: Ch 1, sc in first sc, ch 1, sc in next ch-4 sp, *ch 5, sc in next ch-2 sp, ch 2, sk next 2 dc, sc in next 3 dc, ch 2, sk next ch-2 sp, sc in next ch-2 sp, ch 5, sc in next ch-4 sp, ch 1, sc in next sc, ch 1, sc in next ch-4 sp, rep from * across to last ch-4 sp, sc in last ch-4 sp, ch 1, sc in last sc, turn.

TOP EDGING

Row 1: Ch 1, sc in each sc and in each ch across, turn. (193 sc)

Row 2: Ch 4, sk next sc, dc in next sc, [ch 1, sk next sc, dc in next sc] rep across, turn.

Row 3: Ch 1, sc in each dc and in each ch-1 sp across to turning ch, sc in turning ch lp, sc in 3rd ch of turning ch-4, turn. (193 sc)

Row 4: Ch 1, sc in first 5 sc, ch 3, sk next 3 sc, shell in next sc, ch 3, *sk next 3 sc, sc in each of next 9 sc, ch 3, sk next 3 sc, shell in next sc, ch 3, rep from * across to last 8 sc, sk next 3 sc, sc in each of next 5 sc, turn.

Row 5: Ch 1, sc in each of first 4 sc, ch 4, sk next ch-3 sp, [2 dc, ch 5, 2 dc] in next ch-2 sp, ch 4, *sk next ch-3 sp and next sc, sc in each of next 7 sc, ch 4, sk next ch-3 sp, [2 dc, ch 5, 2 dc] in next ch-2 sp, ch 4, rep from * across to last ch-3 sp, sk last ch-3 sp and next sc, sc in each of next 4 sc, turn.

Row 6: Ch 1, sc in first 3 sc, ch 5, sk next ch-4 sp, 2 dc in next ch-5 sp, [ch 2, 2 dc in same sp] 3 times, ch 5, *sk next ch-4 sp and next sc, sc in next 5 sc, ch 5, sk next ch-4 sp, 2 dc in next ch-5 sp, [ch 2, 2 dc in same sp] 3 times, ch 5, rep from * across to last ch-4 sp, sk last ch-4 sp and next sc, sc in last 3 sc, turn.

Row 7: Ch 1, sc in first 2 sc, ch 5, sk next ch-5 sp, [2 dc, ch 3, 2 dc] in each of next 3 ch-2 sps, ch 5, *sk next ch-5 sp and next sc, sc in next 3 sc, ch 5, sk next ch-5 sp, [2 dc, ch 3, 2 dc] in each of next 3 ch-2 sps, ch 5, rep from * across to last ch-5 sp, sk last ch-5 sp and next sc, sc in each of next 2 sc, turn.

Row 8: Ch 6, sk next ch-5 sp, [2 dc, ch 5, 2 dc] in next ch-3 sp, [ch 1, {2 dc, ch 5, 2 dc} in next ch-3 sp] twice, *ch 6, sk next ch-5 sp and next sc, sc in next sc, ch 6, sk next ch-5 sp, [2 dc, ch 5, 2 dc] in next ch-3 sp, [ch 1, {2 dc, ch 5, 2 dc} in next ch-3 sp] twice, rep from * across to last ch-5 sp, ch 3, sk last ch-5 sp and next sc, dc in last sc to form last ch-6 sp, turn.

Row 9: Ch 1, sc in same sp, ch 4, * [3 dc, p, 3 dc] in next ch-5 sp, rep from * across to last ch-6 sp, ch 4, sc in last ch-6 sp, fasten off.

BOTTOM EDGING

Row 1 (RS): Working in opposite side of foundation ch, attach yarn with sc if first ch, sc in each rem ch across, turn. (193 sc)

Rows 2–9: Rep Rows 2–9 of top edging.

SIDE EDGING

With RS facing, working in ends of rows, attach yarn with sl st in last dc, ch 3, *sk 1 inch, sc in corresponding side of row, p, ch 3, rep from * across, ending with sl st in dc, fasten off.

Rep in same manner on opposite side edge. ★

Diamond Rosebud

*Delicate pink rosebuds carry such promise
and hope of beauty to come. Crochet this lovely
afghan as a special gift for someone you love.*

Design by Diane Poellot

SKILL LEVEL: Intermediate

SIZE: 45 x 58 inches

MATERIALS

- Coats & Clark Red Heart TLC 3-ply worsted weight yarn: 24 oz natural #5017, 19 oz spruce #5662 and 13 oz pale rose #5756
- Size I/9 afghan crochet hook or size needed to obtain gauge
- Tapestry needle

GAUGE

3 knit sts = 1 inch; 4 knit rows = 2 inches

Check gauge to save time.

PATTERN NOTE

Weave in loose ends as work progresses.

PATTERN STITCHES

Tr: Yo hook twice, insert hook around indicated st, yo, draw up a lp, [yo, draw through 2 lps on hook] 3 times.

4-tr cl: Yo hook twice, insert hook around next st 2 rows below, yo, draw up a lp, [yo, draw through 2 lps on hook] twice, [yo hook twice, insert hook around the same st, yo, draw up a lp, {yo,

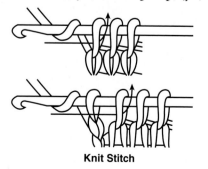

Knit Stitch

draw through 2 lps on hook} twice] 3 times, yo, draw through all 5 lps on hook.

2-tr cl: Yo hook twice, insert around tr 2 rows below, yo, draw up a lp, [yo, draw through 2 lps on hook] twice, yo hook twice, insert hook around next tr 2 rows below, yo, draw up a lp, [yo, draw through 2 lps on hook] twice, yo, draw through all 3 lps on hook.

Knit st: Sk first vertical bar, [insert hook between front and back vertical bars and under horizontal bar on next st (see diagram for assistance), draw up a lp] rep across retaining all lps on hook; Return: yo, draw through first lp on hook, [yo, draw through 2 lps on hook] rep across leaving 1 lp on hook at end of row.

AFGHAN

Row 1: With natural, ch 131, draw up a lp in 2nd ch from hook, retaining all lps on hook, draw up a lp in each rem ch across, yo, draw through first lp on hook, [yo, draw through 2 lps on hook] rep across.

Rows 2–5: Work knit st. At the end of Row 5, fasten off.

Row 6: With spruce, knit st in next 8 sts, sk next st, [work tr around both strands of next st 2 rows below, knit in sk st, knit st in next 3 sts, work tr in same st as previous tr, knit st in next 6 sts] rep across, ending with knit in last st, end st in end st, return, fasten off.

Row 7: With pale rose, knit st in next 10 sts, [4-tr cl, knit in next 10 sts] rep across, ending with

Continued on page 89

Lacy Delight

Whether you wrap your new baby in this exquisite afghan for his or her christening or first visit to Grandma's, you're sure to cherish the image of your precious child in this heirloom keepsake!

Design by Josie Rabier

SKILL LEVEL: Beginner

SIZE: 33 x 51 inches

MATERIALS
- Aunt Lydia's crochet cotton size 10 (1,000 yds per ball): 3 balls white #201
- Size F/5 crochet hook or size needed to obtain gauge
- 20 mauve ribbon roses with lace edge
- 2 yds ⅜₆-inch-wide avocado picot-edged ribbon
- Sewing needle and thread
- Tapestry needle

GAUGE
5 dc = 1 inch; 4 rows = 2 inches
Check gauge to save time.

PATTERN NOTES
Weave in loose ends as work progresses.

Ch 3 counts as first dc throughout.

Work with 2 strands of crochet cotton held tog throughout.

AFGHAN
Row 1 (RS): With 2 strands of white, ch 130, dc in 4th ch from hook, dc in each of next 3 chs, *sk next 3 chs, dc in next ch, [ch 1, dc] 4 times in same ch, sk next 3 chs, dc in each of next 3 chs **, 3 dc in next ch, dc in each of next 3 chs, rep from * across, ending last rep at **, 2 dc in last ch, turn.

Row 2 (WS): Ch 3, dc in same st as beg ch-3, dc in each of next 3 dc, *sk next 2 dc, sc in next ch-1 sp, [ch 3, sk 1 dc, sc in next ch-1 sp] 3 times, sk next 2 dc, dc in each of next 3 dc **, 3 dc in next dc, dc in each of next 3 dc, rep from * across, ending last rep at **, 2 dc in top of ch-3, turn.

Row 3: Ch 3, dc in same st as beg ch-3, dc in each of next 3 dc, *sk next ch-3 sp, dc in next ch-3 sp, [ch 1, dc] 4 times in same ch-3 sp, sk next ch-3 sp and next dc, dc in each of next 3 dc **, 3 dc in next dc, dc in each of next 3 dc, rep from * across, ending last rep at **, 2 dc in top of ch-3, turn.

Rows 4–63: Rep Rows 2 and 3.

TOP BORDER
Row 64: Ch 1, sc in same st as beg ch-1, ch 3, sk next 2 dc, sc in next dc, *ch 3, sk next 2 dc, sc in next dc, ch 3, sk next dc, sc in next dc, ch 3, sk next 2 dc, sc in next dc **, [ch 3, sk next dc, sc in next dc] 3 times, rep from * across, ending last rep at **, ch 3, sk next 2 dc, sc in top of ch-3, turn. (53 ch-3 sps)

Row 65: Ch 3, 2 dc in first ch-3 sp, 3 dc in next ch-3 sp, *[3 dc, ch 3, 3 dc] in next ch-3 sp, [3 dc in next ch-3 sp] twice, rep from * across, ending with 2 dc in last ch-3 sp, 1 dc in last sc, turn. (17 shells)

Row 66: Ch 3, dc in next dc, sk next 2 dc, *dc in each of next 5 dc, [dc, ch 3, dc] in next ch-3 sp, dc in each of next 5 dc sk next 2 dc, rep from * across, ending with dc in last 2 dc, turn.

Row 67: Ch 3, sk next 2 dc, *dc
Continued on page 89

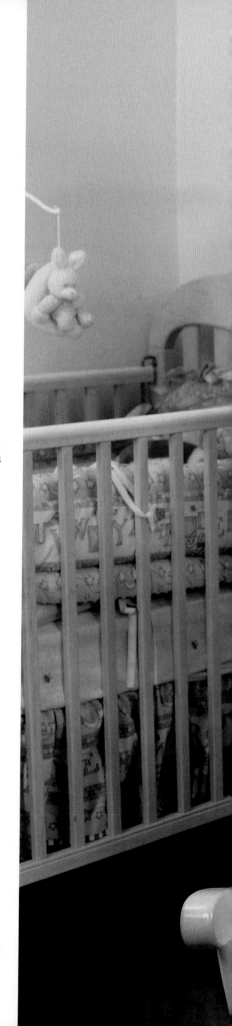

Country Checks & Hearts

Extra-soft and plush yarn gives this charming afghan warmth and coziness! Crochet it as a winter coverlet for a child's bed.

Design by Martha Brooks Stein

SKILL LEVEL: Intermediate

SIZE: 54 x 78 inches

MATERIALS
- Brushed worsted weight yarn: 46 oz white, 15½ oz blue and 10½ oz red
- Size I/9 crochet hook or size needed to obtain gauge
- Tapestry needle

GAUGE
Granny square = 2¾ inches square

Check gauge to save time.

PATTERN NOTES

Weave in loose ends as work progresses.

Ch 2 at beg of a rnd counts as first dc unless otherwise stated.

Sl st to join each rnd in top of beg st.

Make solid-colored granny squares in the following amounts, 258 white, 126 blue and 36 red.

Make 48 two-color granny squares with red and white.

SOLID GRANNY SQUARES

Rnd 1 (RS): Ch 4, sl st to join to form a ring, ch 2, 2 dc in ring, [ch 2, 3 dc in ring] 3 times, hdc in top of beg ch-2 to position hook to start following rnd. (12 dc; 4 ch-2 corner sps)

Rnd 2 (RS): Ch 2, 2 dc in corner sp, [ch 1, {3 dc, ch 2, 3 dc} in corner ch-2 sp] 3 times, ch 1, 3 dc in same corner sp as beg sts, ch 2, join in top of beg ch-2, leaving a

length of yarn, fasten off.

TWO-COLOR GRANNY SQUARES

Rnd 1 (RS): With white, ch 4, sl st to join to form a ring, ch 3, sl st in 2nd ch from hook holding lp made to right of chs, work [2 dc, ch 2, 3 dc] in ring, leaving a 3-inch length, fasten off, with red, leaving a 3-inch length at beg, join with sl st, ch 1, [3 dc, ch 2, 3 dc] in ring, join with sl st in lp of beg ch-3, fasten off. Tie ends of first color change in square knot.

Rnd 2 (RS): In last corner joined, pick up white and join with a sl st, ch 3, sl st in 2nd ch from hook, 2 dc in same corner ch sp, ch 1, [3 dc, ch 2, 3 dc] in next corner ch-2 sp, ch 1, 3 dc in next corner ch-2 sp, leaving a 3-inch length, fasten off, pick up red and join with sl st, ch 1, 3 dc in same corner ch-2 sp as last 3-dc, ch 1, [3 dc, ch 2, 3 dc] in next corner ch-2 sp, ch 1, 3 dc in same corner sp as beg sts, ch 2, join in side lp of beg ch-3, leaving a length of yarn, fasten off. Tie ends of first color change in square knot.

ASSEMBLY

Squares are sewn tog working in back lps only. Following diagrams, sew squares tog as indicated, then sew sections tog.

BORDER

Rnd 1 (RS): Attach white with sl st in back lp of 2nd ch of any ch-2 corner sp, working in back lps for this rnd only, ch 1, sc in same st, *[sc in each of next 3 dc, sc in

Continued on page 90

Flower Cart

Circular motifs worked in springtime-fresh colors make this afghan reminiscent of an old-time flower cart filled with enchanting and fragrant blooms!

Design by Dot Drake

SKILL LEVEL: Intermediate

SIZE: 60 x 62 inches

MATERIALS

- Coats & Clark Red Heart Super Saver worsted weight yarn (8 oz per skein): 3 skeins soft white #316, 1 skein each lilac #353, lavender #358, petal pink #373 and raspberry #375

- Coats & Clark Red Heart Fiesta worsted weight yarn (6 oz per skein): 3 skeins light celery #6615

- Size G/6 crochet hook or size needed to obtain gauge

- Tapestry needle

GAUGE

Circular motif = 8 inches in diameter; 4 sc = 1 inch

Check gauge to save time.

PATTERN NOTES

Weave in loose ends as work progresses.

Sl st to join each rnd unless otherwise stated.

CIRCULAR MOTIF

Note: Make a total of 30 circular motifs with MC of 8 each raspberry and lilac and 7 each of lavender and petal pink.

First triangle

Rnd 1: With MC, ch 5, 3 dc in 5th ch from hook, [ch 3, 4 dc in same 5th ch from hook] twice, ch 3, join in top of beg ch-5, fasten off.

Rnd 2: Attach soft white in any ch-3 sp, ch 3 (counts as first dc throughout), [3 dc, ch 5, 4 dc] in same ch-3 sp, ch 2, [{4 dc, ch 5, 4 dc} in next ch-3 sp, ch 2] twice, join in top of beg ch-3, fasten off.

Rnd 3: Attach light celery in any ch-5 sp, ch 1, 2 sc in same ch-5 sp, [sc in each of next 4 dc, 2 sc in next ch-2 sp, sc in each of next 4 dc, 6 sc in next ch-5 sp] twice, sc in each of next 4 dc, 2 sc in next ch-2 sp, sc in each of next 4 dc, 4 sc in same ch-5 sp as beg 2-sc, join in beg sc, fasten off. (48 sc)

Second triangle

Rep Rnds 1–3 of first triangle, to within joining of Rnd 3. Insert hook in top lp of first sc of working triangle and with WS tog into top lp of previous triangle in 4th sc of any 6-sc corner, sl st triangles tog across 13 sts, fasten off.

Continue to rep 2nd triangle, joining to previous triangle, joining 6th triangle to previous and first to close the circle.

Center

Rnd 1: Attach soft white in any sc at center of motif, ch 1, working around center of circular motif, work 2 sc in each triangle around center, join in beg sc, fasten off. (12 sc)

Border

Rnd 1: Working around outer edge of circular motif, attach soft white in first sc of any triangle, ch 1, [sc in first sc on triangle, {ch 3, sk 1 sc, sc in next sc} 9 times] rep across each of the 6 triangles, sl st to join in beg sc, fasten off.

Following diagram of motif placement, continue to rep Rnd 1 on each circular motif joining edges to previous motifs by working [ch

Continued on page 91

Charleston Garden

Relive the sights and sounds of the old South with this beautiful afghan from 1951. Blooming roses burst from a black background, while a leafy green trim surrounds the entire "garden."

SKILL LEVEL: Intermediate

SIZE:
48 x 69 inches

MATERIALS
- Coats & Clark Red Heart Classic worsted weight yarn: 42 oz black #12, 17.5 oz paddy green #686 and 14 oz berries #973
- Size H/8 crochet hook or size needed to obtain gauge
- Yarn needle

GAUGE
Motif = 8 inches square
Check gauge to save time.

PATTERN NOTES
Weave in loose ends as work progresses.

Join rnds with a sl st unless otherwise stated.

PATTERN STITCHES
Popcorn (pc): 4 dc in indicated st, draw up a lp, remove hook, insert hook in first dc of 4-dc group, pick up dropped lp, draw through st on hook.

Sdc: Yo hook, insert hook in st, yo, draw lp through all lps on hook at one time.

MOTIF
(Make 70)

Rnd 1 (RS): With berries, ch 4, sl st to join to form a ring, ch 3, 3 dc in ring, draw up a lp, remove hook, insert hook in top of beg ch-3, pick up dropped lp, draw through st on hook, ch 3, [pc in ring, ch 3] 3 times, join in top of beg pc. (4 pc; 4 ch-3 sps)

Rnd 2: Ch 1, [sc, 4 dc, sc] in each ch-3 sp around, join in beg sc. (4 petals)

Rnd 3: Ch 1, [sc between petals, ch 4, working in back of petals over first rnd, sc in lower center edge of petal, ch 4] rep around, join in beg sc. (8 ch-4 lps)

Rnd 4: Ch 1, [sc, 5 dc, sc] over each ch-4 lp around, join in beg sc, fasten off. (8 petals)

Rnd 5: Attach paddy green in sc of Rnd 3 between petals of Rnd 4, ch 1, sc in same sc as beg ch-1, *ch 7, sc in 2nd ch from hook, sdc in each of next 2 ch, dc in each of next 3 ch **, sc in next sc to the left between petals in Rnd 3, rep from * around, ending last rep at **, join in beg sc.

Rnd 6: Ch 1, [working on opposite side of foundation ch of leaf, work 5 sc, 3 sc in point of leaf, 5 sc down opposite side of leaf] rep around, join in beg sc, fasten off. (104 sc)

Rnd 7: Attach black in center sc at point of leaf, ch 1, *3 sc in point of leaf, sdc in each of next 2 sc, dc in next sc, sk next 2 sc, yo hook twice, insert hook in last sc on same leaf, yo, draw up a lp, yo, draw through 2 lps on hook, yo, insert hook in first sc on next leaf, yo, draw up a lp, [yo, draw through 2 lps on hook] 4 times, sk next 2 sc, dc in next sc, sdc in each of next 2 sc, rep from * around, join in beg sc.

Rnd 8: Ch 1, *sc in each of next 3 sc, sdc in each of next 2 sts, dc in each of next 3 sts, sdc in each

Continued on page 90

Country Hearts & Roses

Elegant roses and hearts framed in motifs worked with rich shades of cranberry, rose and green with creamy white give this afghan a country feel for Christmas or any season of the year!

Design by Daria McGuire

SKILL LEVEL: Intermediate

SIZE: 48 x 64 inches

MATERIALS

- Coats & Clark Red Heart Classic worsted weight yarn (3.5 oz per skein): 9 skeins off-white #3 (MC), 3 skeins cardinal #917 (A), 1 skein each forest green #689 (B), medium sage #632 (C), light berry #761 (D) and corn-meal #220 (E)
- Coats & Clark Red Heart Super Saver worsted weight yarn: 1 skein each hunter fleck #4389 (F) and bur-gundy fleck #4376 (G)
- Size G/6 crochet hook or size needed to obtain gauge
- Tapestry needle

GAUGE

15 = 4 inches; 2 dc rnds = 1 inch; 15 sts in filet = 4 inches

Check gauge to save time.

PATTERN NOTES

Weave in loose ends as work progresses.

Sl st to join each rnd in top of beg st unless otherwise stated.

PATTERN STITCHES

Puff stitch (puff st): [Yo hook, insert hook in ring, yo, draw up a lp] 4 times, yo, draw through all 9 lps on hook, ch 1 to lock.

Picot (p): Ch 3, sc in first ch of ch-3.

POINSETTIA SQUARES
(Make 6)

Rnd 1 (RS): With E, ch 4, sl st to join to form a ring, [puff st, ch 3] 4 times, join in top of beg puff st, fasten off. (4 puff sts)

Rnd 2 (RS): Attach A in any ch-4 sp, ch 1, [sc, hdc, dc, tr, dtr, tr, dc, hdc, sc] in each ch-4 sp around, join in beg sc. (4 petals)

Rnd 3: Sl st in same st, *sc in each of next 3 sts, [2 dc, p, dc] in next st, sc in each of next 3 sts **, sl st in each of next 2 sts, rep from * around, ending last rep at **, sl st in next st.

Rnd 4: Holding petals forward, [ch 4, sl st in center of ch at base of center of petal on Rnd 2, ch 4, sl st between petals on Rnd 2] rep around. (8 ch-4 lps)

Rnd 5: Holding petals forward, [sc, hdc, dc, tr, dtr, tr, dc, hdc, sc] in each ch-4 sp around, join in beg sc. (8 petals)

Rnd 6: [Sl st in next st, sc in each of next 3 sts, {2 dc, p, dc} in next st, sc in each of next 3 sts, sl st in next st] rep around, fasten off.

Rnd 7 (RS): Holding petals forward, attach B in any sl st of Rnd 4, *ch 10, sc in 2nd ch from hook, sc in next ch, hdc in each of next 2 ch, dc in each of next 2 ch, tr in each of next 3 ch, sl st in next sl st of Rnd 4, rep from * 7 times, join in beg of rnd. (8 leaves)

Rnd 8: [Work 8 dc evenly sp up side of next leaf, 3 dc in st at tip of leaf, 8 dc evenly sp down

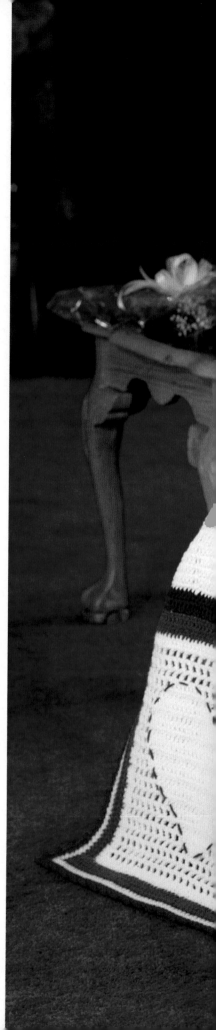

Rocky Mountain High

Snowcapped mountains, cozy cabins nestled in majestic pine forests, and fabulous winter skiing make the Rockies famous around the world! Crochet this collection of handsome and warm afghans to bring a touch of the Rockies into your home!

Textured Aran

Aran patterns, whether knit or crochet, are known for their beautiful textures worked in creamy white yarn. Crochet this lovely example to accent any room in your home!

Design by Angela Tate

SKILL LEVEL: Intermediate

SIZE: 62 x 72 inches plus fringe

MATERIALS

- Coats & Clark Red Heart Super Saver worsted weight yarn (8 oz per skein): 64 oz Aran #313
- Size I/9 crochet hook or size needed to obtain gauge
- Tapestry needle
- Small safety pin or other marker

GAUGE

13 dc and Rnds 1–5 = 5 inches

Check gauge to save time.

PATTERN NOTES

Weave in loose ends as work progresses.

Sl st to join each rnd in top of beg st.

PATTERN STITCH

Popcorn (pc): 5 dc in indicated st, draw up a lp, remove hook, insert hook in first dc of 5-dc group, pick up dropped lp and draw through st on hook, ch 1 to lock.

FIRST STRIP

Rnd 1: Ch 178, 4 dc in 4th ch from hook, *dc in next ch, [pc in next ch, dc in each of next 4 chs] 34 times, pc in next ch, dc in next ch *, 5 dc in last ch, working on opposite side of foundation ch, rep from * to *, join in top of beg ch-3.

Rnd 2: Ch 3 (counts as first dc throughout), dc in same st as beg ch-3, 2 dc in each of next 4 sts, dc in each of next 173 sts, 2 dc in each of next 5 sts, dc in each rem dc around, join in top of beg ch-3.

Rnd 3: Working in front lps for this rnd only, ch 1, reverse sc in each st around, join in beg sc.

Rnd 4: Working in rem free lps of Rnd 2, ch 3, dc in same st as joining, 2 dc in each of next 9 sts, dc in each of next 173 sts, 2 dc in each of next 10 sts, dc in each rem st around, join in top of beg ch-3.

Note: On following rnd, mark 6th and 103rd ch-5 sps with small safety pin or other marker.

Rnd 5: Ch 1, sc in same st as beg ch-1, ch 5, sk next st, [sc in next st, ch 5, sk next st] rep around, join in beg sc, fasten off. (194 ch-5 sps)

SECOND–11TH STRIPS

Rnds 1–4: Rep Rnds 1–4 of first strip.

Note: Marked ch-5 sps on first strip will become center free sps on each end between strips. Beg joining 2nd strip in 4th ch-5 sp to the left of marker and leave 7 free ch-5 sps at each end of strip as subsequent strips are joined.

Joining rnd

Rnd 5: Ch 1, sc in same st as beg ch-1, [ch 5, sk next st, sc in next st] 9 times, [ch 2, sl st in 3rd ch corresponding adjacent ch-5 sp on previous strip, ch 2, sk next st on working strip, sc in next st] 90 times, complete as for first strip, fasten off.

TASSELS

(Make 22)

Cut 20 (12-inch) strands of yarn. Holding tog as one, attach with lark's head knot through center free ch-5 sp on each end of each strip. ★

Kaleidoscope Vista

Beautiful jewel tones create a one-of-a-kind
kaleidoscope effect with this gorgeous afghan!
A solid texture will make it warm and cozy!

Design by Tammy Hildebrand

SKILL LEVEL: Beginner

SIZE: 43 x 64 inches plus fringe

MATERIALS
- Caron Dawn Sayelle worsted weight yarn: 29 oz woodsy ombre #1406 (MC), 5 oz each night sky #0394 (A), fisherman #0336 (B), woodsy green #2028 (C) and rosewine #0469 (D)
- Caron Wintuk worsted weight yarn: 5 oz violet #3081 (E)
- Size J/10 crochet hook or size needed to obtain gauge
- Tapestry needle

GAUGE
5 dc in pattern = 3 inches; 5 pattern rows = 2 inches
Check gauge to save time.

PATTERN NOTE
Weave in loose ends as work progresses.

AFGHAN
Row 1: With A, ch 120, dc in 6th ch from hook, [ch 1, sk next ch, dc in next ch] rep across, fasten off, turn. (59 dc)

Row 2: Working over ch-1 and into skipped chs of previous row, attach MC with sl st in first skipped ch, ch 4 (counts as first dc, ch 1 throughout), dc in next sk ch, [ch 1, dc in next sk ch] rep across, fasten off, turn. (58 dc)

Row 3: Working over ch-1 sps of previous row and into sk sts 2 rows below, attach B with sl st in first st, ch 4, dc in next sk st, [ch 1, dc in next sk st] rep across, fasten off, turn.

Row 4: Working over ch-1 sps of previous row and into sk sts 2 rows below, attach MC with sl st in first sk st, ch 4, dc in next sk st, [ch 1, dc in next sk st] rep across, fasten off, turn.

Row 5: With C, rep Row 3.

Row 6: Rep Row 4.

Row 7: With D, rep Row 3.

Row 8: Rep Row 4.

Row 9: With E, rep Row 3.

Row 10: Rep Row 4.

Row 11: With A, rep Row 3.

Row 12: Rep Row 4.

[Rep Rows 3–12] 18 times, then rep Rows 3–10.

Last Row: Attach A with sl st in first st of 2 rows prior, ch 3 (counts as first dc), [sc in next dc of previous row, dc in next sk dc 2 rows prior] rep across, fasten off.

FRINGE
Work fringe in each st across each short end. Working with MC, cut 2 lengths of yarn each 12 inches long, fold strands in half, insert hook in st, draw fold through st on hook to form a lp, draw cut ends through lp on hook, pull gently to secure. Trim ends evenly. ★

Jeweled Bobbles

Crocheted with a double-ended hook, this striking afghan reveals yet another handsome result of this innovative technique! Crocheted with a black background, bright pink and purple yarn creates a vibrant contrast!

Design by Darla Fanton

SKILL LEVEL: Intermediate

SIZE: 55 x 70 inches

MATERIALS

- Coats & Clark Red Heart TLC Ultra Soft worsted weight yarn: 35 oz black #5012, 15 oz each light purple #5587 and fuchsia #5768
- Size K/10½ (14-inch) double-ended crochet hook or size needed to obtain gauge
- Size K/10½ crochet hook
- Tapestry needle

GAUGE

4 sts = 2 inches; 6 rows = 2 inches

Check gauge to save time.

PATTERN NOTES

Weave in loose ends as work progresses.

If you have difficulty keeping all sts on hook, cap the unused end of hook with either a knitting needle protector or a clean wine cork.

You may want to work opening ch with one size larger hook to get it loose enough since you will be picking up twice in the same ch.

Potential trouble spot: Beg with Row 3 at the point where it says pick up lp in first ch to the left of same vertical bar; make sure you are picking up in the ch and not in the yo that was used to work the lp off the hook.

AFGHAN PANEL
(Make 4)

Row 1: With black, ch 23 loosely, working through back lp only, yo, insert hook in first ch from hook, yo, draw through, yo and draw through the 3 sts on hook, ch 1, [draw up lp in next ch, yo, draw up another lp in same ch, yo, draw through all 3 lps, ch 1] rep across foundation ch; slide all sts to opposite end of hook, turn. (23 lps on hook)

Row 2: To work lps off hook, place light purple on hook with sl knot, working from left to right, draw through first lp, ch 1, [yo, draw through 2 lps on hook (1 lp each color), ch 1] rep across until 1 lp rem on hook, do not turn.

Row 3: With light purple and working right to left, ch 1, sk first vertical bar, [draw up a lp in next vertical bar, yo, draw up a lp in first ch to the left of same vertical bar, yo, draw through all 3 lps on hook, ch 1] rep across, ending with draw up a lp in last vertical bar, ch 1; slide all sts to opposite end of hook, turn. (23 lps on hook)

Row 4: Pick up black, yo and draw through 1 lp on hook, ch 1, [yo, draw through 2 lps on hook, ch 1] rep across until 1 lp rem on hook, do not turn.

Row 5: With black, rep Row 3.

Rows 6 & 7: With fuchsia, rep Rows 2 and 3.

Continued on page 108

Stadium Blanket

Stay warm and cozy during those chilly football games with this extra-long and extra-snuggly afghan! Work it in a combination of variegated yarn in your home-team's colors!

Design by Agnes Russell

SKILL LEVEL: Beginner

SIZE: 49 x 69 inches

MATERIALS
- Lion Brand Homespun yarn (6 oz per skein): 5 skeins each shaker #301 (A) and rococo #311 (B), 6 skeins Edwardian #312 (C)
- Size P/16 crochet hook or size needed to obtain gauge
- Size K/10½ crochet hook
- Tapestry needle

GAUGE
[Sc, ch 3, sc] 4 times = 6 inches
Check gauge to save time.

PATTERN NOTES
Weave in loose ends as work progresses.

Work with 2 strands of yarn held tog throughout unless otherwise indicated.

Afghan is crocheted from center outward.

Fastening off only one color at each color change and adding next color shades afghan. When a color is fastened off, leave a 2-inch length and weave back into same color row. Pattern will indicate which color sequence to use in a two-row sequence, as sequence changes simply fasten off yarn being changed.

PATTERN STITCH
Shell: [Sc, ch 3, sc] in indicated st or sp.

AFGHAN CENTER
First half
Row 1 (RS): With hook size P and 1 strand each A and C held tog, ch 74, shell in 2nd ch from hook, [sk next 2 ch, shell in next ch] 24 times, turn. (25 shells)

Row 2: Ch 1, [shell in ch-3 sp of shell] 12 times, turn.

Row 3: With A and B, rep Row 2.

Row 4: Rep Row 2.

Row 5: With B and C, rep Row 2.

Row 6: Rep Row 2.

Row 7: With A and C, rep Row 2.

Row 8: Rep Row 2.

Rows 9–38: Rep Rows 3–8. At the end of Row 38, fasten off.

Second half
Row 1 (RS): Working in opposite side of foundation ch, attach 1 strand each A and C in same ch at base of end shell of Row 1 of first half, ch 1, shell in same ch as beg ch-1, [sk next 2 ch, shell in next ch] 24 times, turn. (25 shells)

Rows 2–38: Rep Rows 2–38 of first half. At the end of Row 38, do not fasten off, turn.

EDGING
Rnd 39 (RS): With A and B, working across top edge of Row 38, ch 1, sc in ch-3 sp, *[ch 3, sc] 3 times in same ch-3 sp for corner, shell in each of next 23 ch-3 sps, sc in next ch-3 sp, [ch 3, sc] 3 times in same ch-3 sp for corner, working down side edge of rows, shell in side edge of Row 37, [sk 1 row, shell in side edge of next row] 18 times, sk center foundation ch, shell in side edge of Row 1 of next half, [sk 1 row, shell in side edge of next row] 18 times **, sc in next ch-3 sp on Row 38, rep from * to **, sl st to join in beg sc, turn. (134 ch-3 sps)

Rnd 40: Sl st into ch-3 sp, ch 1, shell in same ch-3 sp as beg ch-1, shell in each ch-3 sp around entire outer edge, sl st to join in beg sc, turn.

Rnd 41: With B and C, sl st into ch-3 sp, ch 1, shell in same ch-3 sp as beg ch-1, shell in each ch-3 sp around, working [sc, {ch 3, sc} 3 times] in each center corner ch-3 sp, sl st to join in beg sc, turn.

Rnd 42: Rep Rnd 40.

Rnd 43: Rep Rnd 41.

Rnd 44: Rep Rnd 40, fasten off B only.

Rnd 45 (RS): With hook size K and 1 strand of C, sl st into ch-3 sp, ch 2, sl st in same ch-3 sp, *ch 2, sl st in sp between shells, ch 2 **, [sl st, ch 2, sl st] in ch-3 sp of next shell, rep from * around entire outer edge, ending last rep at **, join in same ch-3 sp as beg sl st, fasten off. ★

Facts About Rocky Mountain States

Utah has the highest literacy rate in the nation.

Wyoming was the first state to give women the right to vote.

Chocolate Layer Cake

Chocolate lovers, here's a fun afghan for your home!
Use your imagination and you'll see layers upon layers
of chocolate cake filled with creamy white frosting!

Design by Kathleen Garen

SKILL LEVEL: Intermediate

SIZE: 42 x 58 inches plus fringe

MATERIALS
- Worsted weight yarn: 24 oz each brown and off-white
- Size I/9 crochet hook or size needed to obtain gauge
- Tapestry needle

GAUGE
5 sc = 1 inch; 6 sc rows = 2 inches
Check gauge to save time.

PATTERN NOTES
Weave in loose ends as work progresses.

Leave a 6-inch length of yarn when fastening off to be worked into fringe.

PATTERN STITCH
Long dc (ldc): Yo hook, insert hook in rem free lp of previous row directly below, yo, draw up a lp, [yo, draw through 2 lps on hook] twice.

AFGHAN
Row 1: With brown, ch 182, hdc in 2nd ch from hook, hdc in each rem ch across, turn. (181 hdc)

Rows 2–4: Ch 1, hdc in each st across, turn.

At the end of Row 4, fasten off.

Row 5: Attach off-white, ch 1, hdc in each hdc across, turn.

Row 6: Ch 1, sc in each st across, fasten off.

Notes: All future rows, except where noted, are worked from RS.

Row 7 (RS): Working in top lp only of each st across, attach brown, ch 1, sc in each st across, fasten off.

Row 8 (RS): Working in top lp only of each st across unless otherwise indicated, attach off-white, ch 1, sc in first st, sk next 2 sts, ldc in rem front lp of each of next 2 sts on row directly below, *[sc in next st, sk next st, ldc in rem front lp of next st on row directly below] 4 times, sc in each of next 7 sts, sk next st, ldc in rem front lp of next st on row directly below, rep from * across, ending with sk next st, ldc in rem front lp of next st on row directly below, sc in next st, fasten off.

Row 9 (RS): Working in top lp only of each st across unless otherwise indicated, attach brown, ch 1, sc in each of next 3 sts, *[sk next st, ldc in rem front lp of next st on row directly below, sc in next st] 4 times, sc in each of next 8 sts, rep from * across, ending with sc in each of next 2 sts, fasten off.

Row 10 (RS): With off-white, rep Row 8.

Row 11 (RS): With brown, rep Row 9.

Row 12 (RS): With off-white, rep Row 8.

Row 13 (RS): With brown, rep Row 9.

Continued on page 109

Country Roses

Rambling wild roses are an added beauty to the rugged Rocky Mountains.
Crochet this reversible beauty of an afghan using a double-ended crochet hook.

Design by Darla Fanton

SKILL LEVEL: Intermediate

SIZE: 43 x 72 inches

MATERIALS

- Coats & Clark Red Heart Soft worsted weight yarn: 17 oz country rose #7775, 16 oz light rose #7722, 10 oz each cranberry #7760 and white #7001
- Size J/10 double-ended crochet hook or size needed to obtain gauge
- Sizes J/10 and K/10½ crochet hooks
- Tapestry needle

GAUGE

With double-ended hook, 4 puffs = 2 inches; 12 rows = 2 inches

Check gauge to save time.

PATTERN NOTES

Weave in loose ends as work progresses.

For ease in making chains loose enough, work beg foundation ch with size K crochet hook.

PATTERN STITCH

Picot (p): Ch 3, sl st in first ch of ch-3.

PANEL A
(Make 5)

Row 1: With country rose, ch 12 loosely, insert double-ended hook under both lps in 2nd ch from hook, yo and draw through ch forming a lp on hook, yo, insert in same ch, yo and draw through, *sk next ch, insert hook in next ch, yo and draw through ch forming a lp on hook, yo, insert

hook in same ch, yo and draw through, keeping all lps on hook, rep from * across foundation ch, slide all sts to opposite end of hook, turn. (19 lps on hook)

Row 2: Place light rose on hook with sl knot, working from left to right draw through first lp, *ch 1, yo, draw through ch and 3 lps (double hook puff made), rep from * across until 1 lp rem on hook, do not turn.

Row 3: With light rose and working right to left, ch 1, *insert hook in last ch-1 sp, yo and draw through keeping lps on hook, yo, insert hook in same sp, yo and draw through, rep from * across, slide all sts to opposite end of hook, turn. (19 lps on hook)

Row 4: Pick up country rose, working from left to right, yo and draw through first lp, *ch 1, yo and draw through ch and 3 lps, rep from * across until 1 lp rem on hook, do not turn.

Row 5: With country rose, rep Row 3.

Row 6: With light rose, rep Row 4.

Rows 7–448: Rep Rows 3–6, ending last rep with Row 4.

Row 449: Bind off in the following manner: With country rose and working right to left, *ch 1, insert hook in next ch-1 sp, yo and draw through, yo, insert hook in same sp, yo and draw through, yo, draw through all 4 lps on hook, rep from * across, fasten off.

EDGING

Rnd 1: With standard hook size J and predominantly country rose side facing, attach white in ch-1

sp at top left corner with a sl st, ch 2, in same sp work a dc holding last lp on hook, yo and draw through both lps on hook, ch 1, in same sp work 2 dc, holding the last lp of each on hook, yo and draw through all 3 lps (standard hook puff made), *ch 1, puff in next sp, rep from * around, working [puff, ch 1, puff] in each corner sp, sl st to join in top of beg ch-2, fasten off. (4 puffs between corner puffs on top and bottom and 112 puffs between corner puffs on each long edge)

Rnd 2: Attach cranberry in top of first puff st of last rnd with sc, [dc, ch 2, dc] in Rnd 1 corner sp, *sc in top of next puff st, dc in end of panel row below ch-1 sp, rep from * across, working [dc, ch 2, dc] in each Rnd 1 corner sp, sl st to join in beg sc, fasten off.

PANEL B
(Make 4)

Work as for panel A, except work edging with predominantly light rose side facing.

ASSEMBLY

Alternating panels A and B and using cranberry, and working through back lps only, whipstitch long edges of panels tog.

BORDER

Rnd 1: With standard hook size J, attach cranberry in any st with a sl st, ch 2 (counts as first hdc), hdc in each st around, working 3 hdc in each corner sp, sl st to join in top of beg ch-2, fasten off.

Rnd 2: Attach white with sc in any st, sc in next st, p, [sc in each of next 2 sts, p] rep around, sl st to join in beg sc, fasten off. ★

Rainbow Ripple

This pretty afghan is a perfect example of using variegated yarn as an accent. Simply select a pretty variegated at your craft store, then choose three colors from the variegated to use as your solids. You'll be pleased with the end result!

Design by Tammy Hildebrand

SKILL LEVEL: Intermediate

SIZE: 44 x 65 inches

MATERIALS
- Coats & Clark Red Heart Super Saver worsted weight yarn: 31 oz painted desert print #303 (MC), 8 oz each Windsor blue #380 (A), country rose #374 (B) and warm brown #336 (C)
- Size P/16 crochet hook or size needed to obtain gauge
- Tapestry needle

GAUGE
5 dc = 2 inches; 4 pattern rows = 3 inches

Check gauge to save time.

PATTERN NOTES
Weave in loose ends as work progresses.

Afghan is worked holding 2 strands of yarn tog throughout.

All even-numbered rows are worked with MC.

AFGHAN

Row 1 (RS): With A, ch 104, dc in 4th ch from hook, dc in each rem ch across, fasten off. (102 dc)

Row 2: With RS facing, attach MC with a sl st in 3rd ch of beg ch-3, ch 3 (counts as first dc throughout), sk next dc, [fpdc around next dc, bpdc around next dc] 3 times, 3 dc in next dc, *[bpdc around next dc, fpdc around next dc] 3 times, bpdc around next dc, sc dec over next 2 dc, [bpdc around next dc, fpdc around next dc] 3 times, bpdc around next dc, 3 dc in next dc, rep from * 4 times, [bpdc around next dc, fpdc around next dc] 3 times, sk next dc, dc in next st, fasten off.

Row 3: With RS facing, working in back lps for this row only, attach B with a sl st in 3rd ch of ch-3, ch 3, sk next st, dc in each of next 6 sts, *3 dc in next st, dc in each of next 7 sts, sk next dc, sc in next sc, sk next dc, dc in each of next 7 sts, rep from * 4 times, 3 dc in next st, dc in each of next 6 sts, sk next st, dc in last st, fasten off.

Row 4: With RS facing, attach MC with a sl st in 3rd ch of ch-3, ch 3, sk next st, [fpdc around next dc, bpdc around next dc] 3 times, 3 dc in next dc, *[bpdc around next dc, fpdc around next dc] 3 times, bpdc around next dc, sc in next sc, [bpdc around next dc, fpdc around next dc] 3 times, bpdc around next dc, 3 dc in next dc, rep from * 4 times, [bpdc around next dc, fpdc around next dc] 3 times, sk next dc, dc in last st, fasten off.

Row 5: With C, rep Row 3.

Row 6: Rep Row 4.

Row 7: With A, rep Row 3.

Row 8: Rep Row 4.

Rows 9–70: Rep Rows 3–8 consecutively, ending last rep after Row 4.

Row 71: With RS facing, working in back lps for this row only, attach C with a sl st in 3rd ch of ch-3, ch 1, sc in same st as beg ch-1, sk next st, sc in each of next 14 sts, *sk next st, 3 dc in next sc, sk next st **, sc in each of next 15 sts, rep from * across, ending last rep at **, sc in each of next 14 sts, sk next st, sc in last st, fasten off.

Row 72: With RS facing, attach MC with a sl st in first sc, ch 1, sc in same st as beg ch-1, sk next st, sc in each of next 12 sts, *sk next st, dc in each of next 3 dc, sk next st **, sc in each of next 13 sts, rep from * across, ending last rep at **, sc in each of next 12 sts, sk next st, sc in last sc, fasten off.

Row 73: With RS facing, attach A with a sl st in first sc, ch 1, sc in same st as beg ch-1, sk next st, sc in each of next 11 sts, *sk next st, sc in each of next 3 dc, sk next st **, sc in each of next 11 sts, rep from * across, ending last rep at **, sc in each of next 11 sts, sk next st, sc in last st, fasten off. ★

Rocky Mountain Trivia

Colorado is the only state in history to turn down the Olympics. The 1976 Winter Olympics were scheduled to be held in Denver. At the last minute, however, 62 percent of state voters chose not to host the Games because of the cost, pollution and population boom it would have caused the area.

Painted Desert

The Southwest is known for arid landscapes with sandy plains, solitary cacti and rocky hills. Its beauty, however, comes in breathtaking ways—vibrant sunsets, and exotic blooms and meadows of flowers after a rainstorm. Capture a sampling of this rugged beauty with this collection of southwestern-style afghans.

Santa Fe Panels

This eye-catching afghan shows off the beauty and simplicity of working with variegated yarn. Rich shades of rose, tan and green blend together seamlessly to create a gorgeous effect!

Design by Eleanor Albano-Miles

SKILL LEVEL: Beginner

SIZE: 46½ x 58 inches

MATERIALS
- Coats & Clark Red Heart Soft worsted weight yarn: 24 oz hollyberry #7946 (A), 10 oz each dark blush #7744 (B) and light wheat #7320 (D) and 5 oz dark yellow green #7675 (C)
- Size J/10 crochet hook or size needed to obtain gauge
- Tapestry needle

GAUGE
3 sc = 1 inch; 4 sc rows = 1 inch

Check gauge to save time.

PATTERN NOTES
Weave in loose ends as work progresses.

Sl st to join each rnd in top of beg st.

PATTERN STITCH
Shell: [2 dc, ch 1, 2 dc] in indicated st.

PANEL
(Make 5)

Row 1: With A, ch 20, sc in 2nd ch from hook, sc in each rem ch across, turn. (19 sc)

Row 2: Ch 3 (counts as first dc throughout), [sk next 2 sts, shell in next st, sk next 2 sts, dc in next st] 3 times, turn. (3 shells)

Row 3: Ch 3, 2 dc in same st as beg ch-3, dc in next ch-1 sp of shell, [shell in next single dc between shells, dc in next ch-1 sp] twice, 3 dc in last dc, turn. (2 shells)

[Rep Rows 2 and 3] 49 times.

Last Row: Ch 1, sc in each st across, fasten off. (19 sc)

PANEL BORDER
Rnd 1 (RS): Attach A to side edge with sc, sc evenly sp around entire outer edge, working 1 sc in ch sps and 2 sc in 3-dc ends of rows, working 3 sc in each corner st, join in beg sc, fasten off.

Rnd 2 (RS): Attach B with a sl st to right corner st at top edge, ch 3, [dc, ch 2, 2 dc] in same corner st, *sk 3 sts, [6 dc in next st, sk next 2 sts, dc in next st, sk next 2 sts] twice, 6 dc in next st, sk next 3 sts, [2 dc, ch 2, 2 dc] in corner st, [sk next 2 sts, dc in next st, sk next 2 sts, 7 dc in next st] rep across side edge to next corner **, [2 dc, ch 2, 2 dc] in corner st, rep from * around, ending last rep at **, join in top of beg ch-3.

Rnd 3 (RS): Working in back lps for this rnd only, ch 1, sc in each st around, working [sc, ch 2, sc] in each corner ch-2 sp, join in beg sc, fasten off.

Rnd 4 (RS): Attach C with sl st in corner ch-2 sp, ch 1, [{2 hdc, ch 2, 2 hdc} in corner ch-2 sp, hdc in each st across edge] rep around, join in top of beg hdc, fasten off.

Rnd 5 (RS): Attach D with sl st in any corner ch-2 sp, ch 3, [dc, ch 2, 2 dc] in same corner ch-2 sp, *dc in each dc across edge **, working [2 dc, ch 2, 2 dc] in each rem corner ch-2 sp, rep from * around, ending last rep at **, join in top of beg ch-3.

Rnd 6 (RS): Ch 1, sc in each st around, working [sc, ch 2, sc] in each corner ch-2 sp, join in beg sc, fasten off.

ASSEMBLY
With WS facing, working through back lps only, with D, whipstitch panels tog.

TRIM
Rnd 1 (RS): Attach D with sc in corner ch-2 sp, ch 1, [{sc, ch 2, sc} in corner ch-2 sp, sc in each st across edge] rep around, join in beg sc, turn.

Rnd 2 (WS): Ch 1, hdc in each st around, working [hdc, ch 2, hdc] in each corner ch-2 sp, join in beg hdc, fasten off. ★

Facts About the Desert States
- *New Mexico has the lowest water-to-land ratio of all 50 states.*
- *Nevada's name comes from a Spanish word, meaning "snow-clad."*
- *Arizona's most abundant mineral is copper. The amount of copper on the roof of the Capitol building is equivalent to 4.8 million pennies.*

Navajo Blanket

Remember the bravery and might of the native Americans with this handsome blanket. A solid single crochet pattern gives this afghan extra warmth and long-lasting durability.

Design by Barbara Shaffer

SKILL LEVEL: Intermediate

SIZE: 48 x 74 inches

MATERIALS

- Coats & Clark Red Heart Super Saver worsted weight yarn: 64 oz aran #313, 12 oz grey heather #400, 11 oz claret #378 and 8 oz black #312
- Size H/8 crochet hook or size needed to obtain gauge
- Tapestry needle

GAUGE

4 sc = 1 inch; 4 rows = 1 inch
Check gauge to save time.

PATTERN NOTES

Weave in loose ends as work progresses.

Work over yarn color not in use.

To changing yarn color, work last sc with working color until 2 lps rem, with next color, yo, draw through rem 2 lps on hook.

AFGHAN

Row 1: With Aran, ch 187, sc in 2nd ch from hook, sc in each rem ch across, fasten off, turn. (186 sc)

Row 2: Attach claret, ch 1, sc in each st across, fasten off, turn.

Row 3: Attach Aran, ch 1, sc in each st across, turn.

Row 4: Attach black, ch 1, [with black, sc in each of next 3 sc, with Aran, sc in each of next 3 sc] 31 times, turn.

Row 5: Ch 1, [with Aran, sc in each of next 3 sc, with black, sc in each of next 3 sc] 31 times, turn.

Row 6: With black, ch 1, [with black, sc in each of next 3 sc, with Aran, sc in each of next 3 sc] 31 times, turn.

Row 7: Rep Row 5, fasten off black, turn.

Row 8: With Aran, ch 1, sc in each st across, fasten off, turn.

Row 9: Rep Row 2.

Rows 10–17: Rep Row 3.

Rows 18–48: With Aran, ch 1, sc in each of next 3 sc, follow chart A changing colors as indicated across 180 sc sts, ending with sc in each of next 3 sc, turn.

Rows 49–56: With Aran, ch 1, sc in each sc across, turn. At the end of Row 56, fasten off.

[Rep Rows 2–56] 4 times.

[Rep Rows 2–10] once, fasten off.

FRINGE

Work fringe in every 3rd st across first and last row of afghan.

Cut 5 lengths of Aran yarn each 18-inches in length. Fold strands in half, insert hook in st, draw strands through at fold to form a lp on hook, draw cut ends through lp on hook, pull to secure. Trim ends to measure 6 inches. ★

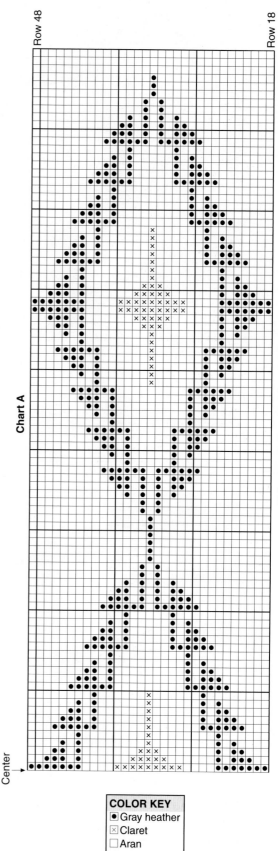

Chart A

Center →

Follow graph Row 18 right to left for first
half of row, then work same row left to
right for 2nd half of row. Work each row
in same manner.

COLOR KEY
- ⊙ Gray heather
- ⊠ Claret
- ☐ Aran

Saguaro Print

Just as the saguaro cactus has captured the imagination of all Americans, so will this understated afghan's colors and design. The more you study it the more depth and interest you'll see!

Design by Katherine Eng

SKILL LEVEL: Intermediate

SIZE: 44 x 64 inches

MATERIALS

- Coats & Clark Red Heart Super Saver worsted weight yarn: 20 oz aspen print #305, 11 oz warm brown #336 and 8 oz light celery #615

- Size H/8 crochet hook or size needed to obtain gauge

- Tapestry needle

GAUGE

Rnds 1–3 = 2½ inches wide x 3½ inches long; center diamond = 5¼ inches

Check gauge to save time.

PATTERN NOTES

Weave in loose ends as work progresses.

Sl st to join each rnd in top of beg st.

Afghan is crocheted from center diamonds outward.

PATTERN STITCHES

Small shell: 5 dc in indicated st.

Large shell: 7 dc in indicated st.

CENTER DIAMOND STRIP

(Make 7 warm brown and 6 light celery)

Notes: *Beg center diamond strip with warm brown, then alternate colors.*

To join diamonds in vertical strip, ch 1, drop lp from hook, draw lp under to over through opposite ch-2 sp, ch 1, continue in pattern.

Rnd 1 (RS): With diamond color, ch 4, sl st to join to form a ring, ch 1, 8 sc in ring, join in beg sc. (8 sc)

Rnd 2: Ch 1, beg in same sc as beg ch-1, [sc in next sc, {sc, ch 2, sc} in next sc, sc in next sc, {sc, ch 3, sc} in next sc] twice, join in beg sc. (12 sc)

Rnd 3: Ch 1, sc in first sc, sc in next sc, {sc, ch 2, sc} in next ch-2 sp, sc in each of next 3 sc, {2 sc, ch 2, 2 sc} in next ch-3 sp (center top of diamond), sc in each of next 3 sc, {sc, ch 2, sc} in next ch-2 sp, sc in each of next 3 sc, {2 sc, ch 2, 2 sc} in next ch-3 sp (center bottom of diamond), sc in next sc, join in beg sc, fasten off. (24 sc)

Rnd 4: Draw up a lp of aspen print in any ch-2 sp, ch 1, [{sc, ch 2, sc} in corner ch-2 sp, sc in each of next 6 sc] 4 times, join in beg sc. (32 sc)

Rnd 5: Ch 1, sc in each sc around, [sc, ch 2, sc] in each corner ch-2 sp, join in beg sc, fasten off. (40 sc)

Rep diamonds alternating center diamond color and joining point to point until all 13 diamonds are joined.

DIAMOND SIDE EDGE TRIM

Note: *Working on side edge of diamond strip, draw up a lp of celery in first sc to the left of ch-2 sp.*

Row 1 (RS): Ch 1, beg in same st as beg ch-1, [sc in each of next 10 sc, {sc, ch 2, sc} in next ch-2 sp, sc in each of next 10 sc] rep across, turn.

Row 2 (WS): Ch 1, dec 1 sc over next 2 sc, *[ch 1, sk 1 sc, sc in next sc] 4 times, ch 1, sk 1 sc, [sc, ch 2, sc] in next ch-2 sp **, [ch 1, sk 1 sc, sc in next sc] 5 times, sk next 2 sc, sc in next sc, rep from * across, ending last rep at **, [ch 1, sk 1 sc, sc in next sc] 4 times, ch 1, sk next sc, dec 1 sc over next 2 sc, fasten off, turn.

Row 3 (RS): Draw up a lp of aspen print in first sc, ch 1, dec 1 sc over first sc and next ch-1 sp, sc in next sc, [sc in next ch-1 sp, sc in next sc] 4 times, *[sc, ch 2, sc] in ch-2 sp **, [sc in next sc, sc in next ch-1 sp] 5 times, sk next 2 sc, [sc in next ch-1 sp, sc in next sc] 5 times, rep from * across, ending last rep at **, sc in next sc, [sc in next ch-1 sp, sc in next sc] 4 times, dec 1 sc over next ch-1 sp and next sc, turn.

Row 4: Rep Row 2.

Rows 5 & 6: With warm brown, rep Row 3 and 4.

Rows 7–10: With aspen print, rep Rows 3 and 4.

Row 11 (RS): Draw up a lp of celery in first sc, ch 2 dc in next ch-1 sp (beg dc dec), *[ch 1, sk 1 sc, dc in next ch-1 sp] 4 times, ch 1, sk 1 sc, [dc, ch 2, dc] in next ch-2 sp **, [ch 1, sk 1 sc, dc in next ch-1 sp] 5 times, sk next 2 sc, dc in next ch-1 sp, rep from *, ending last rep at **, [ch 1, sk 1 sc, dc in next ch-1 sp] 4 times, ch 1, sk 1 sc, dec 1 dc over next ch-1 sp and next sc, turn.

Row 12: Ch 1, sc in first ch-1 sp, *[ch 1, sk 1 dc, sc in next ch-1 sp] 4 times, ch 1, sk 1 dc, [sc, ch 2, sc] in next ch-2 sp **, [ch 1, sk 1 dc, sc in next ch-1 sp] 5 times, sk next 2 dc, sc in next ch-1 sp, rep from *, ending last rep at **, [ch 1, sk 1 dc, sc in next ch-1 sp] 4 times, ch 1, dec 1 sc over next ch-1 sp and next dc, fasten off, turn.

Rows 13–16: With aspen print, rep Rows 3 and 4.

Rows 17 & 18: With warm brown, rep Rows 11 and 12.

Rows 19 & 20: With aspen, rep Rows 3 and 4.

Rows 21–40: Rep Rows 1–20.

Rows 41–44: Rep Rows 1–4.

Rep Rows 1–44 on opposite side of diamond strip.

BORDER

Note: When working across bottom and top on Rnd 1, end of each sc row counts as 1 st. End of each dc row counts as 2 sts. Center ch-2 sp counts as 1 st and each end of 2nd rnd of center diamond at top and bottom counts as 1 st.

Rnd 1 (RS): Draw up a lp of warm brown in first sc of last row, ch 1, working across side, dec 1 sc over first sc and next ch-1 sp, *sk next sc and next ch-1 sp, small shell in next sc, sk next ch-1 sp, sk next sc and next ch-1 sp, sc in next sc, sk next ch-1 sp and next sc, large shell in next ch-2 sp, sk next sc and next ch-1 sp, sc in next sc, sk next ch-1 sp, sk next sc and next ch-1 sp, small shell in next sc, sk next ch-1 sp and sk next sc **, sk 2 center sc between points, dec 1 over next 2 ch-1 sps, rep from * across, ending last rep at **, sk last sc, large shell in end of last row, working across end, [sk 1 st, small shell in next st, sk next st, sc in next st] rep across, ending with sk 1 st, large shell in next st, sk 1 st, rep from beg on opposite side and end, ending after large shell with sl st to join in beg sc.

Rnd 2: Working around each small shell, ch 2, sk 2 dc, [sl st, ch 2, sl st] in next dc, ch 2, sk next 2 dc, sl st in next sc. Working across each large shell, ch 2, sk next 2 dc, sl st in next dc, ch 2, [sl st, ch 3, sl st] in next dc, ch 2, sl st in next dc, ch 2, sk 2 dc, sl st in next sc, ending rnd with sl st in joining sl st of last rnd, fasten off. ★

Birds of the Desert States

Arizona: *Cactus wren*
Nevada: *Mountain bluebird*
New Mexico: *Roadrunner*

Flowers of the Desert States

Arizona: *Saguaro cactus blossom*
Nevada: *Sagebrush*
New Mexico: *Yucca flower*

Twist Stitch Stripes

A unique stitch pattern gives this attractive afghan a knitted look.
Crochet it in soft pastels for a delicate effect, or vibrant shades for more contrast.

Design by Diane Poellot

SKILL LEVEL: Intermediate

SIZE: 45 x 60 inches

MATERIALS
- Coats & Clark Red Heart TLC 3-ply worsted weight yarn: 29 oz natural #5017, 9 oz spruce #5662 and 5 oz peach #5247
- Size J/10 afghan crochet hook or size needed to obtain gauge
- Tapestry needle

GAUGE
3 sts in pattern = 1¼ inches; 2 rows = 1 inch
Check gauge to save time.

PATTERN NOTE
Weave in loose ends as work progresses.

PATTERN STITCHES
Basic forward: Retaining all lps on hook, draw up a lp in each vertical post across row.

Return: Yo, draw through first lp on hook, [yo, draw through 2 lps on hook] rep across until 1 lp remains on hook.

Afghan st: Insert hook from right to left through vertical post of next st, yo and draw lp through.

Twist st: Insert hook from left to right through vertical post of next st (Fig. 1), yo and draw lp through (Fig. 2).

AFGHAN
Row 1: With natural, ch 147, draw up a lp in 2nd ch from hook, work basic forward across, return. (146 sts)

Row 2: Retaining all lps on hook, work [afghan st, twist st] across, return.

Row 3: Rep Row 2, fasten off.

Row 4: Attach spruce, retaining all lps on hook, work [afghan st, twist st] across, fasten off, attach natural, return, fasten off.

Row 5: Attach spruce, retaining all lps on hook work [twist st, afghan st] across, fasten off, attach natural, return, fasten off.

Row 6: Attach peach, retaining all lps on hook, work [twist st, afghan st] across, fasten off, attach natural, return fasten off.

Row 7: Attach peach, retaining all lps on hook, work [afghan st, twist st] across, fasten off, attach natural, return, fasten off.

Rows 8 & 9: Rep Rows 4 and 5.

Row 10: Attach natural, retaining all lps on hook, work [twist st, afghan st] across, return.

Rows 11–14: Rep Row 2.

Rows 15–122: Rep Rows 4–14, ending with Row 12. (11 stripes)

Last row: Inserting hook as for [afghan st, twist st], sl st in each st across, fasten off. ★

Twist Stitch Diagram

1. Insert hook into st from left to right.

2. Yo and draw lp through.

About the Desert States

- *In New Mexico, there are only 12 people per square mile.*
- *Nevada has more mountain ranges than any other state.*
- *Arizona has an official state neckwear: the bola tie.*

Pastel Scrap Delight

Turn those piles of scrap yarn into a delightful baby blanket
with this enchanting pattern! It is sure to be appreciated by the new mother!

Design by Dot Drake

SKILL LEVEL: Beginner

SIZE: 36-inches square

MATERIALS

- Coats & Clark Red Heart Super Saver worsted weight yarn: 12 oz white #311, 6 oz hushaby #930, 3 oz light mint #364, 1 oz each petal pink #373, light blue #381, light coral #327 and pale yellow #322
- Size I/9 crochet hook or size needed to obtain gauge
- Tapestry needle

GAUGE

Motif = 4 inches, 7 dc = 2 inches

Check gauge to save time.

PATTERN NOTES

Weave in loose ends as work progresses.

Sl st to join each rnd in top of beg st.

Work center Rnd 1 of motif with petal pink, light blue, light coral, light mint or pale yellow. Do not use white or hushaby.

PATTERN STITCHES

Front post treble (fptr): Yo hook twice, insert hook front to back to front again around the vertical portion of indicated st, yo, draw up a lp, [yo, draw through 2 lps on hook] 3 times.

Picot (p): Ch 2, sl st in top of last sc.

FIRST MOTIF

Rnd 1 (RS): With center color, ch 4, 15 dc in first ch of beg ch-4, join in top of beg ch-4, fasten off. (16 dc)

Rnd 2: Attach hushaby in any st, ch 3 (counts as first dc throughout), dc in same st as beg ch-3, 2 dc in each rem dc around, join in top of beg ch-3, fasten off. (32 dc)

Rnd 3: Attach white in any dc, ch 1, sc in same dc as beg ch-1, sc in each of next 2 dc, fptr around next dc of Rnd 1 directly below, [sc in each of next 4 dc of Rnd 2, sk next dc of Rnd 1, fptr around next dc of Rnd 1] 7 times, sc in next dc of Rnd 2, join in beg sc. (32 sc; 8 fptr)

Rnd 4: Ch 1, sc in same st as beg ch-1, ch 3, sk next st, [sc in next st, ch 3, sk next st] rep around, join in beg sc, fasten off. (20 ch-3 sps)

SECOND MOTIF

Rnds 1–3: Rep Rnds 1–3 of first motif.

Rnd 4: Ch 1, sc in same st as beg ch-1, *ch 1, sc in next ch-3 sp on previous motif, ch 1, sk next st on working motif, sc in next st on working motif, rep from * 4 times (5 ch lps join to previous motif, ch 3, sk next st, [sc in next st, sk next st, ch 3] rep around, join in beg sc, fasten off.

Continue to rep 2nd motif, joining 8 motifs in a strip, leaving 5 free each side of joining on previous motif.

When working on 2nd strip, join first to rem 5 ch lps on side edge. On 2nd motif of 2nd strip, join to 5 ch lps of previous motif and 5 lps on rem side edge of previous strip of motifs.

Continue making motifs and joining as work progresses until 8 strips of 8 motifs are completed.

BORDER

Rnd 1: Attach white in any ch-3 sp on outer edge, ch 1, sc in same ch-3 sp as beg ch-1, [ch 3, sc in next ch-3 sp] rep around, working ch 4 over each joining of 2 motifs instead of ch 3, ending with ch 1, dc in beg sc.

Rnd 2: Ch 1, sc in same ch-3 sp, ch 3, [sc in next ch-3 sp, ch 3] rep around, join in beg sc.

Rnd 3: Sl st into ch-3 sp, ch 3, 2 dc in same sp as beg ch-3, working around entire outer edge, work 3 dc in each ch-3 sp around and over the 2 ch-3 sps over the ch-4 sp, work dc in ch-3 sp, dc in sc, dc in next ch-3 sp, join in top of beg ch-3.

Rnd 4: Ch 3, dc in each dc around, working [dc in each of next 2 dc, 2 dc in next dc] 9 times evenly sp around each corner, join in top of beg ch-3.

Rnd 5: Ch 3, dc in each dc around, join in top of beg ch-3, fasten off.

Rnd 6: Attach light mint, ch 1, [sc in each of next 2 sts, fptr around next dc of Rnd 4 directly below, sk dc behind fptr] rep around, join in beg sc.

Rnd 7: Ch 1, sc in same sc as beg ch-1, sc in top of fptr, p, [sc in each of next 2 sc, sc in top of next fptr, p] rep around, join in beg sc, fasten off. ★

Pueblo Vistas

Look carefully at this afghan and you can see small adobe huts. Diagonal stitches and a unique blend of colors will make this afghan a handsome accent in your home.

Design by Rosalie DeVries

SKILL LEVEL: Intermediate

SIZE: 46 x 54 inches

MATERIALS

- Worsted weight yarn: 16 oz each soft white (A) and teal (B), 13 oz variegated fall shaded (C)
- Size G/6 crochet hook or size needed to obtain gauge
- Tapestry needle

GAUGE

Rows 1–3 = 2¼ inches

Check gauge to save time.

PATTERN NOTES

Weave in loose ends as work progresses.

Use care when following pattern to place sts as indicated.

PATTERN STITCH

Trtr: Yo hook 4 times, insert hook in indicated st, yo, draw up a lp, [yo, draw through 2 lps on hook] 5 times.

AFGHAN

Row 1 (RS): With A, ch 228, sc in 2nd ch from hook, hdc in each of next 3 chs, sc in next ch, sl st in next ch, *ch 6, sc in 2nd ch from hook, hdc in each of next 3 chs, sc in next ch, sl st in same ch as last sl st, [sc in next ch, hdc in each of next 3 chs, sl st in next ch] twice, rep from * across, fasten off.

Row 2 (RS): With B, draw up a lp in first drawn up lp of previous row, *[trtr in next sl st, catching a strand at center of trtr, work 2 tr in trtr, ch 4, dc in 4th ch from hook, 3 tr in over same strand as last 2-tr sts], sl st in side of next sc of petal, rep between [], sk next 4 sts, sl st in next sc, ch 1, sl st in next sc, rep from * across, fasten off.

Row 3 (RS): With C, draw up a lp in center ch of first ch lp of previous row, *hdc in next dc, hdc in each of next 2 tr, sc in next tr, sl st in next sl st, ch 6, sc in 2nd ch from hook, hdc in each of next 3 chs, sc in next ch, sl st in same sl st as last sl st, sc in next tr, hdc in each of next 2 tr, hdc in base of next dc, sc in center ch of ch lp, trtr in ch-1 sp between columns, sc in center ch of next ch lp, rep from * across, fasten off.

Row 4: With A, rep Row 2.

Row 5: With B, rep Row 3.

Row 6: With C, rep Row 2.

Row 7: With A, rep Row 3.

Rows 8–61: Rep Rows 2–7.

Rows 62–66: Rep Rows 2–6.

Row 67: With A, draw up a lp in center ch, of first ch lp of Row 66, 8 hdc in next dc, hdc in each of next 2 tr, sl st in next sl st, hdc in each of next 2 tr, hdc in base of dc, sl st in center ch of next ch lp, trtr in next ch-1 between columns, sc in center ch of next ch lp, rep from * across, do not fasten off.

FIRST SIDE TRIM

Row 1 (RS): Work 2 sc in same ch as last sc of Row 67, *hdc in next dc, hdc in each of next 2 tr, sc in next tr, sl st in side of next end sc row, sc in same ch as next row end sc, rep from *, ending with 2 sc in same end st, fasten off.

SECOND SIDE TRIM

Row 1 (RS): Draw up a lp of A in drawn up lp of Row 1, 2 sc in drawn up lp of Row 2, *hdc in each of next 3 tr, sc in dc bottom sl st in drawn up lp of next row end, sc in drawn up lp of next row end, rep from *, ending with 2 sc in same first drawn up lp of Row 66, sl st to join in draw up lp of Row 67, do not fasten off.

BORDER

Rnd 1 (RS): Ch 2, [hdc in each st across to center corner st, 3 hdc in center st] rep around, sl st to join in top of beg ch-2.

Rnd 2 (RS): Ch 3, [sk 1 hdc, sc in next hdc, ch 2] rep around, sl st to join in first ch of beg ch-3.

Rnd 3: Sl st into ch sp, ch 1, sc in same ch sp, ch 2, *reverse sc in next ch sp to the right (to the left for left-handed crocheter), ch 2, rep from * around, sl st to join in beg sc.

Rnd 4 (RS): Sl st to center of last lp of Rnd 3, *insert hook from back to front in next lp, sl st in lp, ch 1, insert hook from front to back in next lp, sl st in lp, ch 1, rep from * around with ch-1 lps slightly looser around 4 lps at corners, sl st to join in beg st, fasten off. ★

Desert Sky

A day or so before a desert storm, white puffy clouds spot the vibrant blue sky.
A beautiful and rare event can be captured in this pretty puff stitch granny-square afghan!

Design by Maggie Weldon

SKILL LEVEL: Beginner

SIZE: 51 x 65 inches

MATERIALS
- Bernat Soft Bouclé yarn (5 oz per skein): 5 skeins medium blue #6622 (MC), 3 skeins each angel fish #6901 (CC) and white #6713 (A)
- Size I/9 crochet hook or size needed to obtain gauge
- Tapestry needle

GAUGE
Rnds 1 and 2 = 2¾ inches; square = 6½ inches
Check gauge to save time.

PATTERN NOTES
Weave in loose ends as work progresses.

Sl st to join each rnd in top of beg st.

PATTERN STITCH
Puff st: [Yo hook, insert hook in indicated st, yo, draw up a lp even with hook] 4 times (9 lps on hook), yo, draw through 8 lps on hook, yo, draw through rem 2 lps on hook.

SQUARE A
(Make 32)

Rnd 1 (RS): With MC, ch 4, sl st in first ch to form a ring, ch 3 (counts as first dc throughout), 2 dc in ring, ch 2, [3 dc in ring, ch 2] 3 times, join in top of beg ch-3. (12 dc)

Rnd 2 (RS): Sl st into next ch-2 sp, ch 3, [2 dc, ch 2, 3 dc] in same ch sp as beg ch-3, ch 1, [{3 dc, ch 2, 3 dc} in next ch-2 sp, ch 1] rep around, join in 3rd ch of beg ch-3, fasten off. (24 dc)

Rnd 3 (RS): Attach A in any corner ch-2 sp, ch 1, beg in same corner ch-2 sp as beg ch-1, [sc in corner sp, ch 5, puff st in last sc, sc in same corner sp, ch 3, puff st in last sc, sc in next ch-1 sp, ch 3, puff st in last sc] 4 times, join in beg sc, fasten off. (12 puff sts)

Rnd 4 (RS): Attach CC in any corner ch-5 sp, ch 3, [2 dc, ch 2, 3 dc] in same ch sp, ch 1, [3 dc in next ch-3 sp, ch 1] twice, *[3 dc, ch 2, 3 dc] in next ch-5 sp, ch 1, [3 dc in next ch-3 sp, ch 1] twice, rep from * around, join in top of beg ch-3.

Rnd 5 (RS): Sl st into next ch-2 sp, ch 3, [2 dc, ch 2, 3 dc] in same ch sp, ch 1, [3 dc in next ch-1 sp, ch 1] 3 times, *[3 dc, ch 2, 3 dc] in next ch-2 sp, ch 1, [3 dc in next ch-1 sp, ch 1] 3 times, rep from * around, join in top of beg ch-3, fasten off. (60 dc)

SQUARE B
(Make 31)

Rnds 1 & 2: With CC, rep Rnds 1 and 2 of square A.

Rnd 3: Rep Rnd 3 of square A.

Rnds 4 & 5: With MC, rep Rnds 4 and 5 of square A.

ASSEMBLY
Squares are sewn tog 7 x 9 alternating squares A and B. Beg and ending first row of squares with square A, beg and end 2nd row of squares with square B, continue to rep until all squares are joined.

EDGING
Rnd 1 (RS): Attach MC in any corner, ch 3, [2 dc, ch 2, 3 dc] in same corner sp, ch 1, *[3 dc in next ch-1 sp, ch 1] 4 times, [3 dc in joining of squares, ch 1, {3 dc in next ch-1 sp, ch 1} 4 times] rep across to next corner sp **, [3 dc, ch 2, 3 dc] in next corner sp, ch 1, rep from * around, ending last rep at ** join in top of beg ch-3, fasten off.

Rnd 2 (RS): Attach A in any corner ch-2 sp, ch 1, sc in same sp, *ch 5, puff st in last sc, sc in same corner sp, ch 3, puff st in last sc, [sc in next ch-1 sp, ch 3, puff st in last sc] rep across to next corner ch-2 sp **, sc in corner ch-2 sp, rep from * around, ending last rep at, join in beg sc, fasten off.

Rnd 3 (RS): Attach CC in any corner ch-5 sp, ch 3, [2 dc, ch 2, 3 dc] in same corner sp, ch 1, *[3 dc in next ch-3 sp, ch 1] rep across edge to next corner ch-5 sp, **, [3 dc, ch 2, 3 dc] in next ch-5 sp, ch 1, rep from * around, ending last rep at **, join in top of beg ch-3, fasten off.

Rnd 4 (RS): Attach MC in any corner ch-2 sp, ch 3, [2 dc, ch 2, 3 dc] in same corner sp, ch 1, *[3 dc in next ch-1 sp, ch 1] rep across to next corner ch-2 sp **, [3 dc, ch 2, 3 dc] in corner ch-2 sp, ch 1, rep from * around, ending last rep at **, join in top of beg ch-3, fasten off.

Rnd 5 (RS): Attach A in any corner ch-2 sp, ch 1, *sc in corner ch-2 sp, [ch 4, sk next dc, puff st in next dc, sk next dc, ch 4, sc in next ch-1 sp] rep across edge to next corner ch-2 sp, ch 4, rep from * around, join in beg sc, fasten off. ★

Warm Your Heart

Thick and luscious chenille yarn forms the center of each panel in this gorgeous afghan, as well as the unique "tassels" that make this afghan one-of-a-kind!

Design by Ruth Shepherd

SKILL LEVEL: Intermediate

SIZE: 43½ x 60 inches

MATERIALS

- Lion Brand Chenille Thick & Quick yarn: 7 skeins forest green #131
- Coats & Clark Red Heart Super Saver worsted weight yarn (6 oz per skein): 3 skeins painted desert print #303
- Sizes I/9 and N/15 crochet hooks or sizes needed to obtain gauge
- Tapestry needle

GAUGE

With chenille yarn and N hook, 4 rows = 5 inches, 7 sts = 3½ inches; with worsted weight yarn and I hook, 4 sts = 1 inch; 3 rnds trim = 1½ inches

Check gauge to save time.

PATTERN NOTES

Weave in loose ends as work progresses.

Sl st to join each rnd in top of beg st.

PATTERN STITCH

Shell: [2 dc, ch 2, 2 dc] in indicated st.

AFGHAN STRIP
(Make 7)

Row 1: With forest green and N hook, ch 8, hdc in 2nd ch from hook, hdc in each rem ch across, turn. (7 hdc)

Rows 2–49: Ch 2, hdc in each hdc across, turn.

At the end of Row 49, fasten off.

TRIM

Rnd 1: Working in ends of rows and sts across bottom and top edge, with I hook, attach painted desert print with sl st in side edge of first row, ch 3 (counts as first dc), [dc, ch 2, 2 dc] in same sp, [shell in end of next row] 48 times, shell in first st on short end, [sk next 2 sts, shell in next st] twice, shell in end of each row along side edge, shell in first st on short end, [sk next 2 sts, shell in next st] twice, join in top of beg ch-3.

Rnd 2: Sl st into ch-2 sp, ch 1, [{sc, ch 1, sc} in ch-2 sp, ch 1, hdc between next 2 shells, ch 1] rep around, join in beg sc.

Rnd 3: Sl st into ch-1 sp, [ch 1, sl st in ch sp] rep to center shell on short end, [sc, ch 3, sc] in ch-2 sp of center shell, [ch 1, sl st in next ch sp] rep to center shell on next short end, [sc, ch 3, sc] in ch-2 sp of center shell, [ch 1, sl st in next ch-1 sp] rep to end of rnd, join with sl st in beg sl st, fasten off.

TASSELS
(Make 14)

Row 1: With hook size N, attach forest green with sl st in center ch-3 sp at either end, [ch 4, 3 tr, ch 2, 3 tr, ch 4, sl st] all in same ch sp as beg sl st, fasten off.

Row 2: Attach forest green in ch 2 sp of Row 1, ch 4, *yo hook twice, insert hook in ch-2 sp, yo, draw up a lp, [yo, draw through 2 lps on hook] twice, rep from * 3 times, yo, draw through all 5 lps on hook, ch 4, sl st in same ch-2 sp, fasten off.

Rep Rows 1 and 2 on opposite end of afghan strip.

ASSEMBLY

With tapestry needle and length of painted desert print; sew strips tog on long side edges. ★

Mottoes of the Desert Atates

Arizona: *"Ditat Deus" ("God enriches")*
Nevada: *"All for our country"*
New Mexico: *"Crescit eundo" ("It grows as it goes")*

Desert Medallions

Find a favorite, comfy lounge chair and treat yourself to an afternoon spent crocheting outdoors! This lovely motif afghan will remind you of the prettiest of blue-sky, summer days!

Design by Eleanor Albano-Miles

SKILL LEVEL: Intermediate

SIZE: 49 x 61 inches

MATERIALS

- Coats & Clark Red Classic worsted weight yarn (3½ oz per skein): 12 skeins jockey red #902 (A), 4 skeins each purple #596 (B) and peacock green #508 (C)
- Size J/10 crochet hook or size needed to obtain gauge
- Safety pins
- Tapestry needle

GAUGE

3 sc = 1 inch; 4 sc rows = 1 inch
Check gauge to save time.

PATTERN NOTES

Weave in loose ends as work progresses.

Sl st to join each rnd in top of beg st.

All motifs are worked on RS throughout.

PATTERN STITCH

Fptr: Yo hook twice, insert hook front to back to front again around vertical portion of indicated st, yo, draw up a lp, [yo, draw through 2 lps on hook] 3 times.

FIRST LARGE MOTIF
(Make 32)

Rnd 1 (RS): With A, ch 6, sl st to join to form a ring, ch 1, work 12 sc in ring, join in beg sc. (12 sc)

Rnd 2: Ch 3 (counts as first dc throughout), dc in same st as beg ch-3, 2 dc in each st around, join in top of beg ch-3, fasten off. (24 dc)

Rnd 3: Attach B in any st, ch 1, sc in same st as beg ch-1, *fptr around next st of Rnd 1 directly below, sk st directly behind fptr **, sc in next st, rep from * around, ending last rep at **, join in beg sc, fasten off.

Rnd 4: Attach A with sl st to any st, ch 3, dc in same st as beg ch-3, 2 dc in each st around, join in top of beg ch-3, fasten off. (48 dc)

Rnd 5: Attach C with a sc to first dc of any 2-dc group, *fptr around st directly below (fptr around previous fptr or next sc, whichever is next), sk st directly behind fptr **, sc in next st, rep from * around, ending last rep at **, join in top of beg sc, fasten off.

Rnd 6: Attach A with a sl st to any st above a sc, ch 3, 2 dc in next top of next fptr, [dc in top of next sc, 2 dc in top of next fptr] rep around, join in top of beg ch-3, fasten off. (72 dc)

Rnd 7: Attach B with a sc in 2nd dc of any 2-dc group, fptr around next fptr, [sc in each of next 2 sts, fptr around next fptr] rep around, ending with sc in last st, join in beg sc, fasten off.

Rnd 8: Working in back lps for this rnd only, attach A with a sc, sc in each st around, join in bag sc, fasten off.

SECOND LARGE MOTIF
(Make 31)

Rnds 1 & 2: Rep Rnd 1 of first large motif.

Rnd 3: With C, rep Rnd 3 of first large motif.

Continued on page 135

Indian Gold

Golden medallions encircled by a rich blue made this afghan's beauty timeless. For a more subtle effect, try crocheting it in warm shades of brown with cream.

Design by Anne Halliday

SKILL LEVEL: Beginner

SIZE: 48 x 74 inches

MATERIALS

- Coats & Clark Red Heart Super Saver worsted weight yarn: 24 oz soft navy #387 (MC), 16 oz each cornmeal #320 (A) and gold #321 (B)
- Size I/9 crochet hook or size needed to obtain gauge
- Tapestry needle

GAUGE

Hexagon = 6 x 8½ inches; granny square = 4 inches

Check gauge to save time.

PATTERN NOTES

Weave in loose ends as work progresses.

Sl st to join each rnd in top of beg st.

PATTERN STITCHES

Dtr: To hook 3 times, insert hook in indicated st, yo, draw up a lp, [yo, draw through 2 lps on hook] 4 times.

Dec: *Yo hook, insert hook in next ch sp, yo, draw up a lp, yo, draw through 2 lps on hook *, sk next seam, rep from * to *, yo, draw through all 3 lps on hook.

GRANNY SQUARE

(Make 49)

Rnd 1 (RS): With A, ch 5, sl st to join to form a ring, ch 3 (counts as first dc throughout), 2 dc in ring, ch 3, [3 dc in ring, ch 3] 3 times, join in top of beg ch-3, fasten off.

Rnd 2: Attach B in any corner ch-3 sp, [ch 3, 2 dc, ch 3, 3 dc] in same ch-3 sp, ch 1, [{3 dc, ch 3, 3 dc} in next ch-3 sp, ch 1] rep around, join in top of beg ch-3, fasten off.

Rnd 3: Attach MC in any ch-3 corner sp, [ch 3, 2 dc, ch 3, 3 dc] in same ch-3 sp, ch 1, 3 dc in next ch-1 sp, ch 1, [{3 dc, ch 3, 3 dc} in next corner ch-3 sp, ch 1, 3 dc in next ch-1 sp, ch 1] rep around, join in top of beg ch-3.

HEXAGON

(Make 64)

Rnd 1 (RS): With A, leaving a slight tail at beg, ch 7 (counts as base ch, first tr, ch 2 throughout), in first ch of ch-7 work [tr, ch 2, dtr, ch 5, dtr, ch 2, {tr, ch 2} 3 times, dtr, ch 5, dtr, ch 2, tr, ch 2] all in same ch, join in 5th ch of beg ch-7. (10 ch sps)

Note: Lp a scrap of CC yarn in any st to mark as RS.

Rnd 2: Sl st into ch-2 sp, ch 3, 2 dc in same ch-2 sp, ch 1, 3 dc in next ch-2 sp, ch 1, [3 dc, ch 3, 3 dc] in next ch-5 sp, ch 1, [3 dc in next ch-2 sp, ch 1] 4 times, [3 dc, ch 3, 3 dc] in next ch-5 sp, ch 1, [3 dc in next ch-2 sp, ch 1] twice, join in top of beg ch-3, fasten off. (36 dc; 12 ch sps)

Rnd 3: With RS facing, attach B with sl st in any ch-3 sp, ch 3, [2 dc, ch 3, 3 dc] in same sp, ch 1, [3 dc in next ch-1 sp, ch 1] 5 times, [3 dc, ch 3, 3 dc] in next ch-3 sp, ch 1, [3 dc in next ch-1 sp, ch 1] 5 times, join in top of beg ch-3, fasten off. (42 dc; 14 ch sps)

Rnd 4: With RS facing, attach MC with sl st in any ch-3 sp, ch 3, [2 dc, ch 3, 3 dc] in same ch sp, *[ch 1, 3 dc in next ch-1 sp] twice,

ch 3, 3 dc in next ch-1 sp, ch 1, 3 dc in next ch-1 sp, ch 3, [3 dc in next ch-1 sp, ch 1] twice *, [3 dc, ch 3, 3 dc] in next ch-3 sp, rep from * to *, join in top of beg ch-3, fasten off. (48 dc; 16 ch sps)

TRIANGLE
(Make 14)

Row 1 (RS): With MC, ch 6, [3 dc, ch 3, 3 dc, ch 1, tr] in first ch of beg ch-6, turn. (8 sts; 3 ch sps)

Row 2 (WS): Ch 5 (counts as first tr, ch 1 throughout), 3 dc in next ch-1 sp, ch 1, [3 dc, ch 3, 3 dc] in next ch-3 sp, ch 1, 3 dc in next sp, ch 1, tr in 5th ch of beg ch-5, turn. (14 sts; 5 ch sps)

Row 3: Ch 5, [3 dc in next ch-1 sp, ch 1] twice, [3 dc, ch 3, 3 dc] in next ch-3 sp, ch 1, [3 dc in next ch-1 sp, ch 1] twice, tr in last tr, fasten off. (20 sts; 7 ch sps)

ASSEMBLY
Referring to diagram, working through both lps of each st, with MC, sew 8 hexagons tog to form 8 horizontal strips, beg and ending in center ch of ch-3 sps. Sew 7 squares and 2 triangles to first strip, matching tr sts on triangle to center ch of ch-3 sp on hexagons. Sew next hexagon strip to squares and triangles. Continue sewing rem strips and motifs tog in same manner.

EDGING
Rnd 1 (RS): Attach MC with sl st in ch-3 sp at point A on diagram, ch 4, dc in same sp as beg ch-4, *ch 1, dc in next dc, ch 1, [sk next st, dc in next dc, ch 1] 5 times, [dc, ch 3, dc] in next ch-3 sp, ch 1, [dc in next dc, {ch 1, sk next st, dc in next dc} 5 times, dec, dc in next dc, ch 1, {sk next st, dc in next dc, ch 1} 5 times, {dc, ch 3, dc} in next ch-3 sp, ch 1] 7 times, dc in next dc, ch 1, [sk next st, dc in next dc, ch 1] 5 times, [dc, ch 1, dc] in next ch-3 sp, ch 1, dc in next dc, ch 1, [sk next st, dc in next dc, ch 1] 3 times, [dc in next sp, ch 1, working across next triangle in sps at end of rows, sc in next sp, ch 1,

{sc, ch 1} twice in next sp, sc in next sp, ch 1, sc in center ch, ch 1, sc in next sp, ch 1, {sc, ch 1} twice in next sp, sc in next sp, ch 1, working across next hexagon, dc in next ch sp, ch 1, dc in next dc, ch 1, {sk next st, dc in next dc, ch 1} 3 times] 7 times *, [dc, ch 1, dc] in next ch-3 sp (mark ch-1 sp just made), rep from * to *, join in 3rd ch of beg ch-4.

Rnd 2: Ch 1, [sc, ch 1] twice in next ch-1 sp, *[sc in next ch-1 sp, ch 1] 7 times, [sc, ch 2, sc] in next ch-3 sp, [{ch 1, sc in next ch-1 sp} 6 times, sk next dc, sc in dec, sk next dc, {sc in next ch-1 sp, ch 1} 6 times, {sc, ch 2, sc} in next ch-3 sp] 7 times, ch 1, [sc in next ch-1 sp, ch 1] 7 times, [sc, ch 1] twice in next ch-1 sp *, [sc in next ch-1 sp, ch 1] rep across to next marked sp, [sc, ch 1] twice in marked sp, rep from * to

*, [sc in next ch-1 sp, ch 1] rep across to beg, join in beg sc.

Rnd 3: Ch 1, [sc in next ch-1 sp, ch 1] 9 times, *[sc, ch 2, sc] in next ch-2 sp, [{ch 1, sc in next ch-1 sp} 6 times, sk next sc, sc in next sc, sk next sc, {sc in next ch-1 sp, ch 1} 6 times, {sc, ch 2, sc} in next ch-2 sp] 7 times, ch 1 *, [sc in next ch-1 sp, ch 1] rep across to next ch-2 sp (at first point on opposite end), rep from * to *, [sc in next ch-1 sp, ch 1] rep across to beg, join in beg sc.

Rnd 4: [Sl st in next ch-1 sp, ch 1] 9 times, *[sl st, ch 2, sl st] in next ch-2 sp, [ch 1, {sl st in next ch-1 sp, ch 1} 6 times, sk next sc, sl st in next sc, ch 1, sk next sc, {sl st in next ch-1 sp, ch 1} 6 times, {sl st, ch 2, sl st} in next ch-2 sp] 7 times, ch 1 *, [sl st in next ch-1 sp, ch 1] rep across to next ch-2

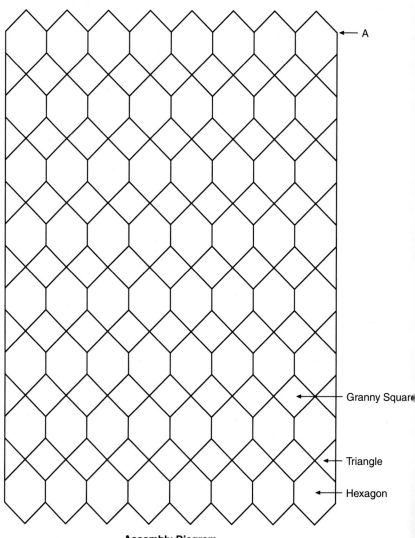

A

Granny Square

Triangle

Hexagon

Assembly Diagram

p (at first point on opposite end), ep from * to *, [sl st in next ch-1 p, ch 1] rep across to beg, join in eg sl st, fasten off. ★

Desert State Wonders

Arizona has 15 popular natural wonders:

The Grand Canyon

Havasu Canyon

Grand Canyon Caves

Lake Powell/Rainbow Bridge

Petrified Forest/Painted Desert

Monument Valley

Sunset Crater

Meteor Crater

Sedona Oak Creek Canyon

Salt River Canyon

Superstition Mountains

Picacho Peak State Park

Saguaro National Park

Chiricahua National Monument

The Colorado River

Desert Medallions
Continued from page 130

Rnd 4: Rep Rnd 4 of first large motif.

Rnd 5: With B, rep Rnd 5 of first large motif.

Rnd 6: Rep Rnd 6 of first large motif.

Rnd 7: With C, rep Rnd 7 of first large motif.

Rnd 8: Rep Rnd 8 of first large motif.

SMALL CIRCLES
(Make 48)

Rnds 1 & 2: With A, rep Rnds 1 and 2 of first large motif. (24 dc)

ASSEMBLY
With WS of large motifs facing, using A and alternating colors of large motifs, whipstitch 2 motifs tog working through back lps of the last rnd of sc across 8 sts. Sew large motifs tog 7 x 9. Use safety pins to hold strips tog while joining to keep edges even.

From WS, place small circles in sps between large motifs and whipstitch 2 or 3 sts to each of the 4 motifs being joined to.

BORDER
Rnd 1 (RS): Attach A to top of any motif on edge, ch 1, *[work 11 sc centered on the side edge of circle, ch 11] rep across edge, on last circle at corner, sc in 11 sc, ch 15, sk next 9 sc of same circle, sc in each of next 11 sc, ch 11, rep from * around entire outer edge, join in beg sc, turn.

Rnd 2 (WS): Ch 1, sc in each sc and each ch around entire outer edge, working [7 sc, ch 2, 7 sc] over each corner ch-15, join in beg sc, turn.

Rnd 3 (RS): Ch 1, sc in each sc around, working [sc, ch 2, sc] in each corner ch-2 sp, join in beg sc, fasten off, turn.

Rnd 4 (WS): Attach B in any corner ch-2 sp, ch 1, *[hdc, ch 2, hdc] in corner ch-2 sp, hdc in each st across edge, rep from * around, join in top of beg hdc, fasten off, turn.

Rnd 5 (RS): With A, rep Rnd 4.

Rnd 6 (WS): With C, rep Rnd 4.

Rnd 7 (RS): With A, rep Rnd 4, do not fasten off, turn.

Rnd 8 (WS): Ch 1, hdc in each hdc around, [hdc, ch 2, hdc] in each corner sp, join in beg hdc, fasten off. ★

Northwest Passage

*Discover the beauty
of the Northwest with
this pretty collection
of warm and cozy
crocheted afghans!
From snowcapped
mountains and alpine
valleys to churning Pacific
shores and towering pines,
the Northwestern states
add rugged beauty and
Western style to
the geography of
the United States.*

Floral Fantasy

Gorgeous meadows filled with enchanting flowers greet you as you climb to the peaks of Washington state's mountains. Capture a sampling of that beauty with this pretty afghan!

Design by Theresa Jones

SKILL LEVEL: Intermediate

SIZE: 46 x 53 inches

MATERIALS
- Coats & Clark Red Heart Super Saver worsted weight yarn (8 oz per skein): 21 oz amethyst #356, 18 oz white #311 and 16 oz paddy green #368
- Size H/8 crochet hook or size needed to obtain gauge
- Tapestry needle

GAUGE
Square = 7 inches; 9 dc = 2 inches
Check gauge to save time.

PATTERN NOTES
Weave in loose ends as work progresses.

Sl st to join each rnd in top of beg st.

PATTERN STITCHES
3-dc cl: [Yo hook, insert hook in indicated st, yo, draw up a lp, yo, draw through 2 lps on hook] 3 times, yo, draw through all 4 lps on hook.

3-tr cl: *Yo hook twice, insert hook in indicated st, yo, draw up a lp, [yo, draw through 2 lps on hook] twice, rep from * twice, yo, draw through all 4 lps on hook.

SQUARE
(Make 42)

Row 1: With amethyst, ch 5, sl st to join in beg ch to form a ring, ch 3 (counts as first dc throughout), 11 dc in ring, join in top of beg ch-3. (12 dc)

Rnd 2: Working in front lps for this rnd only, [ch 10, sl st in same st, ch 15, sl st in next st] rep around, sl st into rem back lp. (24 ch lps)

Rnd 3: Working in rem back lps of Rnd 1, ch 3, dc in same st as beg ch-3, 2 dc in each rem st around, join in top of beg ch-3. (24 dc)

Rnd 4: Ch 3, dc in each of next 4 dc, *[3 dc, ch 3, 3 dc] in next dc for corner **, dc in each of next 5 dc, rep from * around, ending last rep at **, join in top of beg ch-3, fasten off. (44 dc; 4 ch-3 sps)

Rnd 5: Attach paddy green in center dc on any side edge, ch 1, beg in same st, *sc in center dc on side edge, ch 5, [3-dc cl, ch 3, 3-tr cl, ch 3, 3-dc cl] in corner ch-3 sp, ch 5, rep from * around, join in beg sc, fasten off.

Rnd 6: Attach white in any corner 3-tr cl, [ch 3, 2 dc, ch 2, 3 dc] in top of 3-tr cl, *3 dc in next ch-3 sp, 5 dc in each of next 2 ch-5 sps, 3 dc in next ch-3 sp **, [3 dc, ch 2, 3 dc] in top of next 3-tr cl, rep from * around, ending last rep at **, join in top of beg ch-3. (88 dc; 4 ch-2 sps)

Rnd 7: Ch 3, dc in each of next 2 dc, *[2 dc, ch 2, 2 dc] in corner ch-2 sp **, dc in each of next 22 dc, rep from * around, ending last rep at **, dc in each of next 19 dc, join in top of beg ch-3, fasten off. (104 dc; 4 ch-2 sps)

Rnd 8: Attach amethyst in any corner ch-2 sp, ch 1, [3 sc in corner ch-2 sp, sc in each of next 26 dc] rep around, join in beg sc, fasten off. (116 sc)

Continued on page 152

Country Estate

Rounded ripples worked in pretty shades of burgundy, navy and hunter green make this afghan perfect for the den or your husband's favorite armchair!

Design by Laura Gebhardt

SKILL LEVEL: Intermediate

SIZE: 44 x 63 inches

MATERIALS

- Coats & Clark Red Heart Super Saver worsted weight yarn: 15 oz burgundy #376 (B), 13 oz argyle #956 (A), 12 oz soft navy #387 (N) and hunter green #389 (G)
- Size G/6 crochet hook or size needed to obtain gauge
- Tapestry needle

GAUGE

Pattern rep of 1 point and 4 rows = 3 inches

Check gauge to save time.

PATTERN NOTES

Weave in loose ends as work progresses.

Use care as work progresses for proper placement of sts.

PATTERN STITCH

Shell: [2 dc, ch 2, 2 dc] in indicated st.

AFGHAN

Row 1 (WS): With B, ch 246, hdc in 3rd ch from hook, hdc in each of next 6 chs, [hdc, ch 2,

hdc] in next ch, hdc in each of next 8 chs, [sk next 2 ch, hdc in each of next 8 ch, {hdc, ch 2, hdc} in next ch, hdc in each of next 8 ch] rep across, turn.

Row 2: Ch 3 (counts as first dc throughout), dc between 3rd and 4th hdc, ch 3, sk next 2 hdc, dc between last sk hdc and next hdc, dc between next 2 hdc, ch 3, shell in next ch-2 sp, *[ch 3, sk next 2 hdc, dc between last sk hdc and next hdc, dc between next 2 hdc] twice, sk next 6 hdc, dc between last sk hdc and next hdc, dc between next 2 hdc, rep between [ ], ch 3, shell in next ch-2 sp, rep from * to last 8 hdc, rep between [ ], ch 3, sk next 2 hdc, dc between last sk hdc and next hdc, sk next 3 hdc, dc in top of beg ch to form last st, turn. (13 points)

Row 3: Ch 3, sk next dc, working over ch-3 sp, dc in each of next 2 sk hdc in Row 1, [ch 3, sk next 2 dc, working over ch-3 sp, dc in each of next 2 sk hdc in Row 1], ch 3, shell in ch-2 sp of next shell, rep between [ ] twice, *sk next 4 dc, working over next ch-3 sp, dc in next 2 sk hdc in Row 1, rep between [ ], ch 3, shell in ch-2 sp of next shell, rep between [ ]

twice, rep from * across to last st, dc in top of beg ch-3, turn.

Row 4: Ch 3, working over next ch-3 sp, dc in next 2 sk dc in 2nd row below, [ch 3, sk next 2 dc, working over next ch-3 sp, dc in next 2 sk dc 2 rows below], ch 3, shell in ch-2 sp of next shell, rep between [ ] twice, *sk next 4 dc, working over next ch-3 sp, dc in next 2 sk dc 2 rows below, rep between [ ], ch 3, shell in ch-2 sp of next shell, rep between [ ] twice, rep from * across to last 3 sts, sk last 2 dc, dc in top of beg ch-3, turn.

Continuing with B, rep Row 4 twice.

Rep Row 4 in the following color sequence: [3 rows A, 6 rows N, 3 rows A, 6 rows G, 3 rows A, 6 rows B] rep this sequence twice more, ending last rep with only 5 rows of B.

Last row: Ch 2, sk next 2 dc, *[dc in next 2 sk dc 2 rows below, hdc in next 2 dc] twice, [hdc, ch 2, hdc] in next ch-2 sp of shell, [hdc in next 2 dc, dc in next 2 sk dc 2 rows below] twice **, sk next 4 dc, rep from * across, ending last rep at **, sk next 2 dc, dc in top of beg ch-3, fasten off. ★

Northwest Passage flowers

Alaska: *Forget-me-not*
Idaho: *Syringa*
Montana: *Bitterroot*
Oregon: *Oregon grape*
Washington: *Pink rododendron*

Seashells

Unlike the white sands of the Southern states, much of the sand in the Northwest is slightly gray in color. Capture the beauty of the rugged Northwest coast with this ruffled motif afghan!

SKILL LEVEL: Intermediate

SIZE: 52 x 62 inches

MATERIALS
- Caron Sayelle worsted weight yarn (3½ oz per skein): 12 skeins dark gray #364, 6 skeins each dark dusty rose #424 and dusty rose #423, 4 skeins canyon coral #2051, 3 skeins peach #305
- Size H/8 crochet hook or size needed to obtain gauge
- Tapestry needle

GAUGE
Motif = 8½ inches square
Check gauge to save time.

PATTERN NOTES
Weave in loose ends as work progresses.

Join rnds with a sl st unless otherwise stated.

When a rnd begs with a dc, simply ch 3 for first dc.

PATTERN STITCH
Shell: Work 5 dc around vertical portion of indicated st.

SQUARE
(Make 42)

Rnd 1: With dark gray, ch 4, sl st to join to form a ring, ch 1, 8 sc in ring, join in beg sc, turn. (8 sc)

Rnd 2: Ch 1, 2 sc in same sc as joining, [sc in next sc, 3 sc in next sc] 3 times, sc in next sc, sc in same sc as first 2 sc, join in beg sc, turn. (16 sc)

Rnd 3: Ch 1, 2 sc in same sc as beg ch-1, [sc in each sc across to center sc of next corner, 3 sc in corner sc] rep around, ending with 1 sc in same sc as first 2 sc, join, turn. (24 sc)

Rnd 4: Rep Rnd 3, fasten off, do not turn. (32 sc)

Rnd 5: Attach peach in any center sc of any corner, ch 1, sc in same st as beg ch-1, *sk next st, 3 dc in next st, sk next st, sc in next st, rep from * around, ending with sk last st, join in beg sc, fasten off, do not turn.

Rnd 6: Attach dark gray in center corner st, *[dc, ch 1, tr, ch 1, dc] in center corner st, sc in top of center dc of next 3-dc group, 3 dc in next sc, sc in top of center dc of next 3-dc group, rep from * around, join, fasten off, turn.

Rnd 7: Attach peach in first dc of any corner, ch 1, sc in same dc, *ch 1, sc in next tr, ch 1, sc in next dc, work a shell around vertical post of center dc of next 3-dc group of 2nd rnd down (peach), sc in center dc of next 3-dc group of previous rnd, shell around vertical post of center dc of next 3-dc group of 2nd rnd down (peach) **, sc in first dc of next corner, rep from * around, ending last rep at **, join, fasten off, turn.

Note: *The sts of the following rnd are worked in sts of 2nd round down (dark gray).*

Rnd 8: Attach canyon coral in top corner tr inserting hook through center of sc previously worked in
Continued on page 153

Festive Pine & Holly

Red, green and white pine trees create a crocheted forest surrounded by holly berries and leaves! Crochet this festive afghan to add to the Christmas season!

Design by Sandra Abbate

SKILL LEVEL: Intermediate

SIZE: 47 x 58 inches

MATERIALS
- Coats & Clark Red Heart Super Saver worsted weight yarn (* oz per skein): 2 skeins each burgundy #376, hunter green #389 and soft white #316
- Size H/8 crochet hook or size needed to obtain gauge
- Tapestry needle

GAUGE
4 sts = 1 inch; 1 stripe = 2¼ inches
Check gauge to save time.

PATTERN NOTES
Weave in loose ends as work progresses.

Change yarn color by working last 2 lps of old color with new color.

AFGHAN
Row 1: With burgundy, ch 146, dc in 5th ch from hook, *ch 4, sk next 4 ch, sc in next ch, ch 4, sk next 4 ch **, 3 dc in next ch, rep from * across, ending last rep at **, 1 dc in each of last 2 ch, turn.

Row 2: Ch 2 (counts as first dc throughout), [2 dc in next dc, ch 3, sc in next sc, ch 3, 2 dc in next dc, dc in next dc] rep across, turn.

Row 3: Ch 2, dc in next dc, *2 dc in next dc, ch 2, dc in next sc, ch 2, 2 dc in next dc **, dc in each of next 3 dc, rep from * across, ending last rep at **, dc in each of next 2 dc, turn.

Row 4: Ch 2, dc in each of next 2 dc, 2 dc in next dc, *ch 1, sk next dc, 2 dc in next dc **, dc in each of next 5 dc, 2 dc in next dc, rep from * across, ending last rep at **, dc in each of next 3 dc, changing to hunter green in last st, turn.

Row 5: Ch 1, sc in first dc, [ch 4, 3 dc in next ch-1 sp, ch 4, sk next 4 dc, sc in next dc] rep across, turn.

Row 6: Ch 1, sc in first sc, [ch 3, 2 dc in next dc, dc in next dc, 2 dc in next dc, ch 3, sc in next sc] rep across, turn.

Row 7: Ch 4 (counts as first dc, ch 2), *2 dc in next dc, dc in each of next 3 dc, 2 dc in next dc, ch 2, dc in next sc **, ch 2, rep from * across, ending last rep at **, turn.

Row 8: Ch 3, *2 dc in next dc, dc in each of next 5 dc, 2 dc in next dc **, ch 1, sk next dc, rep from * across, ending last rep at **, tr in 2nd ch of beg ch-4, changing to soft white in last st, turn.

Row 9: Ch 2, dc in tr, *ch 4, sk next 4 dc, sc in next dc, ch 4 **, 3 dc in next ch-1 sp, rep from * across, ending last rep at **, 2 dc in top of turning ch, turn.

Maintaining color sequence with next 3 rows with soft white, [rep Rows 2–9] 11 times, then rep Rows 2–4, fasten off. (9 stripes burgundy and 8 each hunter green and soft white)

HOLLY EDGING
Note: *Edging is made in 4 strips and sewn to afghan.*

SHORT STRIP
(Make 2)
First leaf
Row 1: With hunter green, ch 4, 4 dc in 4th ch from hook, turn. (5 dc)

Row 2: Ch 3 (counts as first dc throughout), 2 dc in same st as beg ch-3, dc in each of next 3 dc, 3 dc in last dc, turn. (9 dc)

Row 3: Ch 1, sl st in first 4 dc, ch 3, 2 dc in same st as beg ch-3, dc in next dc, 3 dc in next dc, leaving rem sts unworked, turn. (7 dc)

Row 4: Ch 3, 2 dc in same st as beg ch-3, dc in each of next 5 dc, 3 dc in last dc, turn. (11 dc)

Row 5: Ch 1, sl st in each of next 4 dc, ch 3, 2 dc in same st as beg ch-3, dc in each of next 3 dc, 3 dc in next dc, leaving rem sts unworked, turn. (9 dc)

Row 6: Ch 1, sl st in each of next 3 dc, ch 2, [yo, insert hook in next dc, yo, draw up a lp, yo, draw through 2 lps on hook] 4 times, yo, draw through all 5 lps on hook, ch 1 to lock (5-dc cl), turn.

Row 7: Ch 1, sc in top of cl, turn. (1 sc)

Second leaf
Row 1: Ch 3, 4 dc in sc, turn. (5 dc)

Rows 2–7: Rep Rows 2–7 of first leaf.

Continue to rep 2nd leaf until 12 leaves are completed, then fasten off.

HEADER
Row 1: Attach soft white with sl st in first point (on end) of first leaf, ch 4 (counts as first dc, ch 1), dc in same st as beg ch-4, *ch 2, sc in next point, ch 2, hdc in next point, ch 2, holding back last lp of each tr on hook, tr in last point on working leaf and first point on next leaf, yo, draw through all 3 lps on hook, ch 2,
Continued on page 152

Dream Puff Delight

Here's a perfect baby gift for the expectant mother when you don't know if the baby is a boy or girl. Worked with the crochet-on-the double technique, this afghan is reversible and oh-so-soft!

Design by Darla Fanton

SKILL LEVEL: Intermediate

SIZE: 34 x 39 inches

MATERIALS

- Coats & Clark Red Heart Baby Soft sport weight yarn: 9 oz white twinkle #8001, 5 oz light blue #7815 and 4 oz light rose #7722
- Size K/10½ double-ended crochet hook or size needed to obtain gauge
- Size J/10 crochet hook
- Tapestry needle

GAUGE

8 puff sts = 2 inches; 8 rows = 2 inches

Check gauge to save time.

PATTERN NOTES

Weave in loose ends as work progresses.

If you have difficulty keeping all of the sts on the hook, cap the unused end of hook with either a knitting needle protector or a clean wine cork.

When picking up a lp in horizontal st, insert hook under top lp only.

In order to achieve proper tension on foundation ch you may find it easier to use a hook one size larger.

AFGHAN

Row 1: With light blue, ch 126 loosely, working through back lp only, draw up lp in 2nd ch from hook, yo, draw up a lp in same ch, [draw up a lp in next ch, yo, draw up a lp in same ch] rep across foundation ch, slide all sts to opposite end of hook, turn. (376 lps on hook)

Row 2: To work off lps, place white on hook with sl knot, working from left to right draw sl knot through first lp, [yo, draw through 4 lps] rep across until 1 lp rem on hook, do not turn.

Row 3: With white, working right to left, ch 1, sk first vertical bar, [draw up a lp in next horizontal st, yo, draw up a lp in same st] rep across, slide all sts to opposite end of hook, turn. (376 lps on hook)

Rows 4 & 5: With light rose, rep Rows 2 and 3.

Row 6: With white twinkle, yo and draw through 1 lp, [yo, draw through 4 lps on hook] rep across until 1 lp rem on hook, do not turn.

Row 7: Rep Row 3.

Row 8: With light blue, rep Row 6.

Row 9: With light blue, rep Row 3.

Rows 10 & 11: Rep Rows 6 and 7.

Row 12: With light rose, rep Row 6.

Rows 13–160: Rep Rows 5–12 until piece measures approximately 38 inches ending with Row 8.

Row 161: To bind off, with light blue, working right to left, ch 1, sk first vertical bar, [draw up a lp in next horizontal st, yo, draw up a lp in same horizontal st, yo and draw through all 4 lps on hook] rep across, transfer rem light blue lp to size J hook to work edging, fasten off light rose and white twinkle.

FIRST SIDE EDGING

Ch 2, in same sp as last puff was worked, [draw up a lp, yo, draw up a lp, yo, draw through all 4 lps on hook] rep evenly sp along side edge, ending with ch 2, join with sl st in first foundation ch, fasten off.

SECOND SIDE EDGING

Attach light blue with sl st in same ch as first puff st on foundation ch, ch 2, in end of white twinkle row, [draw up a lp, yo, draw up a lp in same st, yo, draw through all 4 lps on hook] rep evenly sp along side edge, ending with ch 2, join with sl st in top of first puff on Row 161, fasten off.

BORDER

Rnd 1: Attach light blue with sl st in any st, ch 2, hdc evenly sp around entire outer edge, working [2 hdc, ch 2, 2 hdc] in each corner, sl st to join in top of beg ch-2, fasten off.

Rnd 2: With light rose, rep Rnd 1

Rnd 3: Attach white twinkle in any corner ch-2 sp, ch 1, [3 sc in corner ch-2 sp, sc in each st across side edge] rep around, join in beg sc, fasten off. ★

Diamond Strip

*Perfect for taking on an afternoon sail, this
handsome afghan has high-class style!*

Design by Maggie Weldon

SKILL LEVEL: Beginner

SIZE: 45 x 65 inches

MATERIALS

- Coats & Clark Red Heart Classic worsted weight yarn (3.5 oz per skein): 7 skeins soft navy #853 (MC), 5 skeins off-white #3 (A) and 6 oz honey gold #645 (B)

- Size I/9 crochet hook or size needed to obtain gauge

- Tapestry needle

GAUGE

6 dc = 2 inches; 4 rows = 1 inch; one diamond = 1¼ inches square; strip = 5 inches wide
Check gauge to save time.

PATTERN NOTES

Weave in loose ends as work progresses.

Sl st to join each rnd in top of beg st.

STRIP

(Make 10)

Center diamonds

Row 1: With A, ch 8, dc in 4th ch from hook, dc in each of next 3 chs, leaving last ch unworked, turn.

Row 2: Ch 3, dc in next 3 sts.

Rep Rows 1 and 2 until 24 diamonds are completed, ending last rep with Row 2, ch 1, fasten off.

Border

Rnd 1: With any side facing and working across 1 side of all diamonds, attach MC in ch-1 sp at either end of diamonds, ch 4 (counts as first tr throughout), 11 tr in same ch, ** sc in point of first diamond, *7 tr in ch-1 sp between next 2 diamonds, sc in next point, rep from * 22 times, 12 tr in end ch, working on opposite side, rep from **, omitting last 12 tr, join in 4th ch of beg ch-4, fasten off. (394 sts)

Rnd 2 (RS): Attach B in first tr of Rnd 1, ch 1, sc in same st, *[ch 1, sc in next tr] 11 times, ch 1, sk next st, [sc in next st, ch 1, sk next st] rep across to first tr of end 12-dc group **, rep from *, ending at **, join in beg sc, fasten off. (208 ch-1 sps)

Rnd 3 (RS): Attach A in first ch-1 sp of Rnd 2, ch 3 (place a marker on beg ch-3), dc in same ch-1 sp as beg ch-3, 2 dc in each ch-1 sp around, join in top of beg ch-3, fasten off. (416 dc)

Rnd 4 (RS): Attach MC in sp before marked ch-3 of Rnd 3, ch 3, dc in same sp, [2 dc in sp between next 2-dc group] twice, [3 dc in sp between next 2-dc group] 6 times, [2 dc in sp between next 2-dc group] 100 times, [3 dc in sp between next 2-dc group] 6 times, [2 dc in sp between next 2-dc group] 97 times, join in top of beg ch-3, fasten off. (428 dc)

ASSEMBLY

Sew long sides of strips tog. ★

Blue Cables

Narrow stripes of color make this an easy afghan to adapt to any decor. In our sample, pretty shades of light and dark blue form cables set apart by rows of creamy white.

Design by Tammy Hildebrand

SKILL LEVEL: Beginner

SIZE: 45 x 65 inches

MATERIALS

- Lion Brand Homespun textured yarn: 42 oz hepplewhite #300 (MC), 29 oz each Williamsburg #321 (A) and colonial #302 (B)
- Size N/15 crochet hook or size needed to obtain gauge
- Tapestry needle

GAUGE

2 dc = 1 inch; 3 rows = 2 inches
Check gauge to save time.

PATTERN NOTES

Weave in loose ends as work progresses.

Work with 2 strands of yarn held tog throughout afghan.

PATTERN STITCH

Fptr: Yo hook twice, insert hook front to back to front again around vertical post of tr directly below, yo, draw up a lp, [yo, draw through 2 lps on hook] 3 times.

AFGHAN

Row 1 (RS): With 2 strands of MC, ch 89, dc in 4th ch from hook, dc in next ch, [ch 1, sk next ch, dc in each of next 3 chs] 21 times, fasten off.

Row 2 (RS): Holding 1 strand each A and B tog, attach with sc in first st, ch 1, sk next st, sc in next st, working over ch-1 in skipped chs, [tr in next sk ch, sc in next st, ch 1, sk next st, sc in next st] 21 times, fasten off.

Row 3 (RS): Attach 2 strands of MC with sc in first st, working over ch-1 in sk sts, dc in next sk st, sc in next st, [ch 1, sk next st, sc in next st, dc in next sk st, sc in next st] 21 times, fasten off.

Row 4 (RS): Holding 1 strand of each A and B tog, attach with sc in first st, ch 1, sk next st, sc in next st, [fptr around next tr directly below, sc in next st, ch 1, sk next st, sc in next st] 21 times, fasten off.

Rep Rows 3 and 4 until afghan measures 65 inches.

Last Row (RS): Attach 2 strands of MC with sc in first st, working over ch-1 in sk sts, dc in next sk st, [sc in each of next 3 sts, dc in next sk st] 21 times, fasten off.

FRINGE

Work fringe in each st on each short side of afghan. For each fringe, cut a strand of each A and B each 12 inches long. Holding both strands tog, fold in half, insert hook in st, draw strands through at fold to form a lp on hook, draw cut ends through lp on hook, pull to secure. Trim all ends evenly. ★

Northwestern States

- *In 1867, the United States purchased Alaska for $7.2 million, or 2 cents per acre, from Russia.*
- *Idaho's Seven Devils' Peaks include Heaven's Gate Lookout, where sightseers can look into four states.*

Floral Parade

One of Southern California's most anticipated annual events is the Rose Bowl Parade. Breathtaking floats created entirely of flowers enchant and amaze the world over. Crochet this exquisite afghan to celebrate this event!

Design by Dot Drake

SKILL LEVEL: Intermediate

SIZE: 54 x 76 inches

MATERIALS

- Coats & Clark Red Heart Super Saver worsted weight yarn (8 oz per skein): 3 skeins light raspberry #774 (R), 2 skeins each petal pink #373 (P), light celery #615 (MC) and soft white #316 (W) and 1 skein lilac #353 (L)

- Coats & Clark Red Heart Fiesta yarn (6 oz per skein): 2 skeins light celery #6615 (LC)

- Size G/6 crochet hook or size needed to obtain gauge

- Tapestry needle

GAUGE

Large motif = 10 inches; small motif = 4 inches; 7 sc = 2 inches

Check gauge to save time.

PATTERN NOTES

Weave in loose ends as work progresses.

Sl st to join each rnd in top of beg st.

LARGE MOTIF
(Make 35)

Note: *Rnds 1–5 of large motif are worked from outer edge to center.*

Rnd 1 (RS): With LC, ch 96, using care not to twist ch, sl st to join to form a ring, ch 3 (counts as first dc throughout), dc in each of next 3 ch, ch 10, [dc in each of next 4 ch, ch 10] rep around, join in top of beg ch-3, fasten off. (96 dc; 24 ch-10 lps; 24 groups 4-dc)

Rnd 2 (RS): Attach R in 2nd dc of any 4-dc group between ch-10 lps of previous rnd, ch 3, dc in next dc, dc in 2nd and 3rd dc of next 4-dc between ch-10 lps, ch 10, *[dc in 2nd and 3 dc of next 4-dc group between ch-10 lps] twice, ch 10, rep from * around, join in top of beg ch-3. (48 dc; 12 ch-10 lps; 12 groups 4-dc)

Rnd 3 (RS): Attach P in 2nd dc of any 4-dc group between ch-10 lps of previous rnd, ch 3, dc in next dc, ch 10, [dc in 2nd and 3rd dc of next 4-dc group between ch-10 lps, ch 10] rep around, join in top of beg ch-3, fasten off. (24 dc; 12 ch-10 lps; 12 groups 2-dc)

Rnd 4: Attach W in first dc of previous rnd, ch 3, dc in next dc, ch 10, [dc in each of next 2 dc between ch-10 lps, ch 10] rep around, join in top of beg ch-3, fasten off. (24 dc; 12 ch-10 lps; 12 groups 2-dc)

Place motif on a flat surface with Rnd 1 on outside of circle, remembering that Rnd 1 has 24 ch-10 lps and all rem rnds have 12 ch-10 lps. *Insert hook in lp to right on Rnd 1, insert hook in next lp of Rnd 1 to the left, draw this lp through first lp, insert hook in lp directly above of Rnd 2, draw this lp through lp on hook, draw lp directly above of Rnd 3 through lp on hook, draw lp directly above of Rnd 4 through lp on hook, remove hook. Rep from * until all lps around motif are chained toward center of motif. (12 ch lps at center)

Rnd 5: Working at center of motif, with MC, leaving a length at beg, ch 4, sc in 1 lp at center, ch 3, sl st in first ch of beg ch-4, [ch 3, sc in next ch lp at center, ch 3, sl st in same first ch of beg ch-4] rep around, leaving a length of yarn, fasten off; secure beg and ending lengths to keep center secure.

Rnd 6 (RS): Working in opposite side of foundation ch, attach W in any st, sl st in each ch around.

Rnd 7: Ch 1, sc in same st as beg ch-1, ch 3, sk next sl st, [sc in next sl st, ch 3, sk next sl st] rep around, join in beg sc, fasten off.

Rnd 8: Working in back of previous rnd, attach P in first sk st, ch 1, sc in same st, *ch 5, sc in next sk sl st, rep from * 4 times, ch 7 **, sc in next sk sl st, rep from * around, ending last rep at **, join in beg sc, fasten off. (8 ch-7 lps; 40 ch-5 lps)

Rnd 9: Attach MC in first ch-5 sp, ch 1, beg in same ch sp, [2 sc in each of next 5 ch-5 sps, {2 sc, ch 2, 2 sc} in next ch-7 sp] rep around, join in beg sc. (112 sc; 8 ch-2 sps)

Rnd 10: Ch 1, sc in each sc around and 2 sc in each ch-2 sp, join in beg sc, fasten off. (128 sc; 16 sc each side edge)

SMALL MOTIF
(Make 32)

Rnd 1: With L, ch 5, 3 dc in first ch of ch-5, [ch 3, 4 dc in same first ch of beg ch-5] 3 times, ch 3, sl st to join in top of beg ch-5, fasten off.

Rnd 2: Attach W in ch-3 sp, ch 3, [3 dc, ch 5, 4 dc] in same ch-3 sp, ch 2, [{4 dc, ch 5, 4 dc} in

Continued on page 17

Springtime Shells

Springtime flowers burst forth in vibrant hues of yellow and lavender in the West, as well as most regions of the country. Celebrate their arrival with this quick-to-crochet delight!

Design by Tammy Hildebrand

SKILL LEVEL: Beginner

SIZE: 44 x 67 inches

MATERIALS
- Lion Brand Terryspun textured yarn: 14 oz each lavender #144 (A), citron #157 (B) and seaspray #123 (C)
- Size P/16 crochet hook or size needed to obtain gauge
- Tapestry needle

GAUGE
[1 shell, 1 sc] twice = 5½ inches
Check gauge to save time.

PATTERN NOTES
Weave in loose ends as work progresses.

Complete afghan is crocheted from the RS.

PATTERN STITCH
Shell: [2 dc, ch 1, 2 dc] in indicated st.

AFGHAN
Row 1 (RS): With A, ch 62, sc in 2nd ch from hook, sk next ch, shell in next ch, sk next ch, sc in next ch, [sk next ch, shell in next ch, sk next ch, sc in next ch] rep across, fasten off. (16 sc; 15 shells)

Row 2 (RS): Attach B in first sc, ch 3 (counts as first dc throughout), dc in same st as beg ch-3, sc in next ch-1 sp, [shell in next sc, sc in next ch-1 sp] 14 times, 2 dc in last sc, fasten off.

Row 3 (RS): Attach C in top of beg ch-3, ch 1, sc in same dc as beg ch-1, shell in next sc, [sc in next ch-1 sp, shell in next sc] 14 times, sc in last dc, fasten off.

Row 4: With A, rep Row 2.

Row 5: With B, rep Row 3.

Row 6: With C, rep Row 2.

Row 7: With A, rep Row 3.

[Rep Rows 2–7] 10 times.

FRINGE
Working across foundation ch, fringe is attached in the base of each sc st and in the base of each shell. Working across last row of afghan, fringe is worked in each ch-1 sp of each shell and in each sc. Cut 1 strand of each color 14 inches in length. Fold 3 strands in half, insert hook in indicated st, draw fold through st on hook to form a lp, draw cut ends through lp on hook, pull gently to secure. ★

Pacific States Flowers

California: *California poppy*
Hawaii: *Hibiscus or pua aloalo*

Paneled Throw

With both sides equally beautiful, this lovely lavender-hued afghan is a reversible treasure. This pattern is perfect for those just learning to use a double-ended crochet hook!

Design by Dot Drake

SKILL LEVEL: Beginner

SIZE: 38 x 58 inches

MATERIALS

- Coats & Clark Red Heart Fiesta yarn (6 oz per skein): 3 skeins each light periwinkle #6347 and lavender #6358 and 2 skeins baby white #6301
- Size J/10 double-ended crochet hook or size needed to obtain gauge
- Size G/6 crochet hook
- 11 large safety pins
- Tapestry needle

GAUGE

Panel = 4¾ inches wide before border

Check gauge to save time.

PATTERN NOTE

Weave in loose ends as work progresses.

PANEL A
(Make 2)

Row 1: With hook size J and lavender, ch 20, draw up a lp in 2nd ch from hook, retaining all lps on hook, draw up a lp in each ch across, slide all sts to opposite end of hook, turn. (20 lps on hook)

Row 2: To work lps off, place light periwinkle on hook with a sl knot, working from left to right, draw through first lp, [yo, draw through 2 lps on hook] rep across until 1 lp rem on hook, do not turn.

Row 3: With light periwinkle, working right to left, draw up a lp in each vertical bar across, slide

all sts to opposite end of hook, turn. (20 lps on hook)

Row 4: With lavender, rep Row 2.

Row 5: With lavender, rep Row 3.

Row 6: With light periwinkle, rep Row 2.

Row 7: With light periwinkle, rep Row 3.

Rows 8–194: Rep Rows 4–7, ending last rep with Row 2.

Row 195: Sl st in each vertical bar across, fasten off.

PANEL B
(Make 3)

Row 1: With baby white, rep Row 1 of panel A.

Row 2: With light periwinkle, rep Row 2 of panel A.

Row 3: With light periwinkle, rep Row 3 of panel A.

Row 4: With baby white, rep Row 2.

Row 5: With baby white, rep Row 3.

Row 6: With light periwinkle, rep Row 2.

Row 7: With light periwinkle, rep Row 3.

Rows 8–194: Rep Rows 4–7, ending last rep with Row 2.

Row 195: Sl st in each vertical bar across, fasten off.

BORDER

On a flat surface, arrange 3 B panels side by side with the one in the center with the predominantly baby white side facing up. Place one panel A on each side of the 3 B panels, with one panel having

the predominantly lavender side facing up, and the other panel having the predominantly light periwinkle side facing up. Mark RS of each panel with a safety pin.

Row 1 (RS): With strip facing and G hook, attach baby white, sl st evenly sp down long side edge of strip, turn.

Row 2 (WS): Ch 2 (counts as first hdc), working in top lps only, hdc in each st across, turn, fasten off.

Row 3 (RS): Attach lavender, ch 1, sc in same st, ch 10, [sc in each of next 3 hdc, ch 10] rep across edge, ending with sc in last st, fasten off.

Rep Rows 1–3 on each long side of each panel.

ASSEMBLY

Maintaining established order of panels, place first panel on a flat surface, working on outer left edge, insert hook in first ch lp, draw 2nd ch lp through first lp, [draw next ch lp through ch lp on hook] rep to top of panel. Remove hook and temporarily secure rem lp with safety pin. Rep in same manner on outer right edge of 5th panel.

Place first and 2nd panels on flat surface. Beg at bottom edge, insert hook in first ch lp on strip to the right, draw first ch lp on panel to the left through lp on hook, [insert hook in next ch lp on right, draw through lp on hook, insert hook in next ch lp on left, draw through lp on hook] continue to rep, alternating sides as work progresses to top of panel. Remove hook and temporarily secure lp

Continued on page 171

Surf & Sand

This attractive afghan is reminiscent of rippling waves washing up on a serene beach in a constant, soothing rhythm.

Design by Darla Fanton

SKILL LEVEL: Intermediate

SIZE: 46 x 69 inches

MATERIALS

- Coats & Clark Red Heart TLC 3-ply worsted weight yarn (5 oz per skein): 21 oz sand #5335, 17 oz medium blue #5823, 6 oz each light blue #5815 and natural #5017
- Size P/16 double-ended crochet hook or size needed to obtain gauge
- Size N/15 crochet hook
- Tapestry needle

GAUGE

Strip before edging = 4¼ inches; 4 rows = 1 inch

Check gauge to save time.

PATTERN NOTES

Weave in loose ends as work progresses.

Sl st to join each rnd in top of beg st.

To pick up a lp under vertical bar, insert hook under indicated bar, yo and draw through.

Carry unused yarn along side edge by bringing it to the front and working over it for beg ch-1 on odd numbered rows.

STRIP A
(Make 6)

Row 1: With hook size P and medium blue, ch 14, working through back lps only, insert hook in 2nd ch from hook, yo and draw through, *insert hook in back lp of next ch, yo and draw through, rep from * across foundation ch, retaining all lps on hook, slide all sts to opposite end of hook, turn. (14 lps on hook)

Row 2: To work lps off hook, place sand on hook with sl knot, working from left to right draw through first lp, *yo, draw through 2 lps (1 lp of each color), rep from * across until there is 1 lp left on hook, do not turn.

Row 3: With sand, working right to left, ch 1, sk first vertical bar, [yo, pick up lp under next vertical bar] twice, [with yarn to the front, insert hook under next 2 vertical bars tog and draw up a lp] 4 times, [yo, draw up a lp under next vertical bar] twice, draw up a lp under last vertical bar, slide all sts to opposite end of hook, turn. (14 lps on hook)

Row 4: With light blue, rep Row 2.

Row 5: With light blue, rep Row 3.

Row 6: Pick up sand, yo and draw through 1 lp, [yo, draw through 2 lps] rep across until 1 lp rem on hook, do not turn.

Row 7: Rep Row 3.

Row 8: With natural, rep Row 2.

Row 9: With natural, rep Row 3.

Row 10: Rep Row 6.

Row 11: Rep Row 3.

Row 12: With medium blue, rep Row 6.

Row 13: With medium blue, rep Row 6.

Row 14: Rep Row 6.

Row 15: Rep Row 7.

Continued on page 170

Wavy Shells

Create a stunning accent piece for your home with this wavy shell afghan! Work it in contrasting colors as shown for more impact, or two similar tones for a soothing effect.

Design by Melissa Leapman

SKILL LEVEL: Beginner

SIZE: 49 x 59 inches

MATERIALS
- Elmore-Pisgah's Peaches & Cream cotton (2½ oz per skein): 10 skeins peacock #19 (A) and 11 skeins white #1 (B)
- Size H/8 crochet hook or size needed to obtain gauge
- Tapestry needle

GAUGE
In pattern, each shell = 1¼ inches wide

Check gauge to save time.

PATTERN NOTES
Weave in loose ends as work progresses.

Sl st to join each rnd in top of beg st.

PATTERN STITCH
Shell: [{Dc, ch 1} 3 times and dc] in indicated st.

AFGHAN
Row 1 (RS): With A, ch 186, [dc, ch 1, dc] in 4th ch from hook, *sk next 3 ch, sc in each of next 7 ch, sk next 3 ch **, shell in next ch, rep from * across, ending last rep at **, [dc, ch 1, 2 dc] in last ch, turn.

Row 2 (WS): Ch 1, sc in each st and each ch-1 sp across, ending with sc in turning ch, change to B, turn.

Row 3: Ch 1, sc in first sc, working in back lps only, sc in next 3 sc, *sk next 3 sc, shell in next sc, sk next 3 sc **, working in back lps only, sc in next 7 sc rep from *

across, ending last rep at **, working in back lps only, sc in each of next 3 sts, working through both lps, sc in next sc, turn.

Row 4: Ch 1, sc in each st and each ch-1 sp across, change to A, turn.

Row 5: Ch 3 (counts as first dc throughout), [dc, ch 1, dc] in first sc, *sk next 3 sc, working in back lps only, sc in each of next 7 sc, sk next 3 sc **, shell in next sc, rep from * across, ending last rep at **, ending with, [dc, ch 1, 2 dc] in last sc, turn.

Rep Rows 2–5 until throw measures approximately 58 inches, ending with a Row 5 of pattern.

Last Row: Ch 1, sc in first 2 dc, sc in next ch-1 sp, sc in next dc, *hdc in each of next 7 sc **, [sc in next dc, sc in next ch-1 sp] 3 times, sc in next dc, rep from * across, ending last rep at **, sc in next dc, sc in next ch-1 sp, sc in next dc, sc in top of turning ch, fasten off.

BORDER
Rnd 1 (RS): Attach B with sl st to upper right hand corner, ch 1, [181 sc across edge of afghan, 3 sc in corner st, 219 sc across edge, 3 sc in corner st] rep around, join in beg sc.

Rnd 2: Ch 4 (counts as first dc, ch 1), *sk next sc, dc in next sc, ch 1, rep from * around, working [dc, ch 1] 3 times in each center corner sc, join in 3rd ch of beg ch-4.

Rnd 3: Ch 1, sc in each dc and each ch-1 sp around, working 3 sc in each corner dc, join in beg sc.

Rnd 4: Ch 1, [sc in each of next 2 sc, ch 3, sl st in last sc] rep around, join in beg sc, fasten off. ★

Yo-Yo Strips

If you enjoy crocheting motifs, then you'll love creating this one-of-a-kind afghan! Small yo-yos worked in a plush variegated are then joined into strips and worked into panels.

Design by Tammy Hildebrand

SKILL LEVEL: Intermediate

SIZE: 42 x 64 inches

MATERIALS
- Lion Brand Homespun textured yarn: 29 oz hepplewhite #300 (MC) and 25 oz tudor #315 (CC)
- Size I/9 crochet hook or size needed to obtain gauge
- Tapestry needle

GAUGE
First yo-yo = 1¾ inches across; strip = 6 inches wide

Check gauge to save time.

PATTERN NOTES
Weave in loose ends as work progresses.

Sl st to join each rnd in top of beg st.

PATTERN STITCHES
V-st: [Dc, ch 1, dc] in indicated st.

Cross: Sk next 2 sts, dc in next st, ch 3, working backward over dc just made, dc in skipped st.

Cross joining: Sk next 2 sts, dc in next st, ch 1, sl st in center ch of corresponding ch-3 sp on previous strip, ch 1, working backward over dc just made, dc in sk st.

STRIPS
(Make 7)
First yo-yo
Rnd 1 (RS): With CC, ch 3, sl st to join to form a ring, ch 3 (counts as first dc throughout), [6 dc, ch 1, 7 dc] in ring, ch 1, join in top of beg ch-3, fasten off.

Second yo-yo
Rnd 2 (RS): With CC, ch 3, sl st to join to form a ring, ch 3, 6 dc in ring, sl st in ch-1 sp of previous yo-yo, 7 dc in same ring, ch 1, sl st to join in top of beg ch-3, fasten off.

Rep 2nd yo-yo until a strip of 24 yo-yos are joined tog.

BORDER
Rnd 1 (RS): Attach MC with sl st in center ch-1 sp at either end of strip, ch 4 (counts as first dc, ch 1), dc in same ch-1 sp, working in back lps for this rnd only, *V-st in next st, [sk next st, V-st in next st] twice, [sk next 2 sts after ch-1 sp on next yo-yo, V-st in next st, sk next st, V-st in next st] 23 times, sk next st, V-st in next st *, V-st in next ch-1 sp, rep from * to *, join in 3rd ch of beg ch-4.

Rnd 2 (RS): Ch 3, dc in each st and each ch-1 sp around entire outer edge, join in top of beg ch-3, fasten off.

JOINING
First strip
Rnd 3 (RS): Attach CC with sl st in sp just before center st at either end of strip, [work crossover next 3 sts, sl st in sp before next st] 101 times, work crossover next 3 sts, join with sl st in same sp as beg sl st, fasten off.

Second strip
Rnd 3 (RS): Attach CC with sl st in sp just before center st at either end of strip, [work crossover next 3 sts, sl st in sp before next st] twice, work cross over joining next 3 sts, sl st in sp before next st] 46 times, [work crossover next 3 sts, sl st in sp before next st] 52 times, work crossover next 3 sts, join with sl st in same sp as beg sl st, fasten off.

Continue to rep 2nd strip, joining strip to previous strip until all 7 are joined tog. ★

Pacific States Mottoes

California: *"Eureka!"* (*"I have found it!"*)
Hawaii: *""Ua mau ke ea o ka aina I ka pono."*
(*"The life of the land is perpetuated in righteousness."*)

Lacy Shells

*Here's a pattern you can pick up and put down with ease!
A simple shell pattern worked in a solid cotton yarn
makes a lighter-weight afghan perfect for warmer climates!*

Design by Melissa Leapman

SKILL LEVEL: Beginner

SIZE: 45 x 55 inches

MATERIALS
- Elmore-Pisgah's Peaches & Cream cotton (2½ oz per skein): 20 skeins tea rose #42
- Size H/8 crochet hook or size needed to obtain gauge
- Tapestry needle

GAUGE
In pattern, 2 shells = 1¾ inches wide

Check gauge to save time.

PATTERN NOTES
Weave in loose ends as work progresses.

Sl st to join each rnd in top of beg st.

PATTERN STITCH
Shell: 4 dc in indicated st.

AFGHAN
Row 1 (RS): Ch 207, sc in 2nd ch from hook, sc in next ch, *ch 1, sk next 4 ch, shell in each of next 2 ch, ch 1, sk next 4 ch, sc in each of next 2 ch, rep from * across, turn.

Row 2 (WS): Ch 3 (counts as first dc), dc in next sc, *ch 4, sk next 3 dc, sc in next 2 dc, ch 4, dc in next 2 sc, rep from * across, turn.

Row 3 (RS): Ch 1, sc in each of next 2 dc, *ch 1, shell in each of next 2 sc, ch 1, sc in next 2 dc, rep from * across, ending with ch 1, shell in each of next 2 sc, ch 1, sc in next dc, sc in top of turning ch, turn.

Rep Rows 2 and 3 until throw measures approximately 55 inches, ending with Row 3 of pattern.

Last row: Ch 3, dc in next sc, *ch 3, sk next 3 dc, sc in next 2 dc, ch 3, dc in each of next 2 sc, rep from * across, fasten off.

BORDER
Rnd 1 (RS): Attach yarn with sl st to upper right-hand corner, ch 1, [work 171 sc across edge of afghan, 3 sc in corner st, 205 sc across edge of afghan, 3 sc in corner st] rep around, join in beg sc.

Rnd 2: Ch 1, sc in same sc as beg ch-1, [ch 2, sk next sc, sc in next sc] rep around, working [sc, ch 2] twice in each center corner sc, join in beg sc.

Rnd 3: Sl st into ch-2 sp, ch 1, [{sc, ch 3, sc} in next ch-2 sp] rep in each ch-2 sp around, join in beg sc, fasten off. ★

Pacific States Birds

California: *California valley quail*
Hawaii: *Nene*

Row 16: With light blue, rep Row 6.

Row 17: Rep Row 5.

Row 18: Rep Row 6.

Row 19: Rep Row 3.

Row 20: With natural, rep Row 6.

Rows 21–228: Rep Rows 9–20, ending last rep at end of Row 12.

Row 229: To bind off, with medium blue and working right to left, ch 1, sk first vertical bar, [insert hook under next vertical bar, yo and draw through st, yo and draw through both lps on hook] twice, [with yarn to the front, insert hook under next 2 vertical bars, yo and draw through, yo and draw through both lps on hook] 4 times, [insert hook under next vertical bar, yo and draw through st, yo and draw through both lps on hook] twice, insert hook under last vertical bar, yo and draw through, yo and draw through both lps on hook, transfer rem lp to hook size N to work edging.

EDGING

With predominantly sand side facing and working in ends of rows, work 170 sc evenly sp along side edge ending at foundation ch, fasten off. Attach medium blue in opposite end of foundation ch and work 170 sc evenly sp on rem side edge, fasten off.

STRIP B
(Make 5)

Row 1: With medium blue, ch 14, working through back lps only, insert hook in 2nd ch from hook, yo and draw through, [insert hook in back lp of next ch, yo and draw through] rep across retaining all lps on hook, slide all sts to opposite end of hook, turn. (14 lps on hook)

Row 2: To work off lps, place sand on hook with sl knot, working from left to right draw through first lp, [yo, draw through 2 lps on hook (1 lp of each color)] rep across until 1 lp rem on hook, do not turn.

Row 3: With sand, working right to left, ch 1, sk first vertical bar, [yo, draw up a lp under next vertical bar] twice, [with yarn to the front, insert hook under next 2 vertical bars tog and draw up a lp] 4 times, [yo, draw up a lp under next vertical bar] twice, draw up a lp under last vertical bar, slide all sts to opposite end of hook, turn. (14 lps on hook)

Row 4: With natural, rep Row 2.

Row 5: With natural, rep Row 3.

Row 6: Pick up sand, yo and draw through 1 lp, [yo, draw through 2 lps on hook] rep across until 1 lp rem on hook, do not turn.

Row 7: Rep Row 3.

Row 8: With light blue, rep Row 2.

Row 9: With light blue, rep Row 3.

Row 10: Rep Row 6.

Row 11: Rep Row 3.

Row 12: With medium blue, rep Row 6.

Row 13: With medium blue, rep Row 3.

Row 14: Rep Row 6.

Row 15: Rep Row 7.

Row 16: With natural, rep Row 6.

Row 17: Rep Row 5.

Row 18: Rep Row 6.

Row 19: Rep Row 3.

Row 20: With light blue, rep Row 6.

Rows 21–228: Rep Rows 9–20, ending last rep with Row 12.

Row 229: To bind off, with medium blue, working right to left, ch 1, sk first vertical bar, [insert hook under next vertical bar, yo and draw through st, yo and draw through both lps on hook] twice, [with yarn to front, insert hook under next 2 vertical bars, yo and draw through, yo and draw through both lps on hook] 4 times, [insert hook under next vertical bar, yo and draw through st, yo and draw through both lps on hook] twice, insert hook under last vertical bar, yo and draw through, yo and draw through both lps on hook, transfer rem lp to size N hook to work edging.

EDGING

With predominantly sand facing and working in ends of rows, work 170 sc evenly sp along edge ending at foundation ch, fasten off. Attach medium blue in opposite end of foundation ch and work 170 sc evenly sp across opposite edge, fasten off.

JOINING

Alternating strips A and B with predominantly sand facing and Row 1 of strip A at bottom and Row 1 of strip B at top, with medium blue, working in back lps only, sew strips tog.

BORDER

Rnd 1 (RS): Attach medium blue in any st, ch 1, sc evenly sp around entire outer edge, working 3 sc in each corner st, join in beg sc.

Rnd 2: Ch 1, sc evenly sp around, working 3 sc in each center corner sc and inc 2 or 3 sts at top of each curve and dec 2 or 3 sts on inner curves as needed to keep project flat and maintain the wave effect, join in beg sc.

Rnd 3: Rep Rnd 2, fasten off. ★

Floral Parade
Continued from page 156

next ch-3 sp, ch 2] rep around, join in top of beg ch-3, fasten off.

Rnd 3: Attach MC in any ch-5 sp, ch 1, [6 sc in ch-5 sp, sc in each of next 4 dc, 2 sc in next ch-2 sp, sc in each of next 4 dc] rep around, join in beg sc, fasten off. (64 sc; 16 sc each side edge)

ASSEMBLY
Using diagram as a guide and working in back lps only, sew large motifs tog 5 x 7 motifs, working across 16 sc sts of side edge.

Using diagram as a guide, sew small motifs between large motifs.

BORDER
Rnd 1 (RS): Attach R in first sc of any corner 2 sc worked in ch-2 sp of Rnd 10, ch 1, *sc in each of next 2 sc on point of motif, ch 6,

drop lp from hook, insert hook in previous sc, pick up dropped lp and draw through st on hook, working over ch-6 lp, [3 sc, ch 3, sl st in first ch of ch-3 for p] 3 times and 3 sc over ch-6 lp, sc in each sc until next 2-sc group worked at a point, rep from * around, working ch-6 lps over 3rd and 4th sc sts of each small motif; at each joining of two motifs, ch 1, sk last sc of working motif and first sc of next motif, sc in next sc, join in beg sc, fasten off . ★

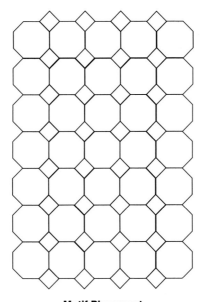

Motif Placement

MOTIF KEY

◯ Large motif
◇ Small motif

Paneled Throw
Continued from page 160

with safety pin. Turn panels over to make sure no ch lps were missed. Continue to rep in this manner until all panels are joined.

With lavender and tapestry needle, tack end of each lp at top of afghan to secure.

TRIM
Note: *Rep Rows 1–3 on each top and bottom of afghan.*

Row 1 (RS): With G hook, attach lavender in edge, ch 1, sc evenly sp across front panel, [ch 6, sk over ch lp joining between panels, sc evenly sp across next panel] rep across, turn.

Row 2: Ch 2, hdc in each sc and each ch across, turn.

Row 3: Ch 12, [sl st in 3rd ch from hook, ch 10, sl st in next 2 hdc, ch 12] rep across, ending with ch 10, sc in last hdc, fasten off. ★

Pacific State Facts
Each Hawaiian island is represented by flowers and colors:

Nihau: *Pupu Shell—White*
Kauai: *Mokihana (green berry)—Purple*
Oahu: *Ilima—Yellow*
Maui: *Lokelani (pink cottage rose)—Pink*
Molokai: *White kukui blossom—Green*

Lanai: *Kaunaoa
(yellow and orange air plant)—Orange*
Kahoolawe: *Hinahina
(beach heliotrope)—Gray*
Big Island of Hawaii: *Lehua ohia—Red*

General Instructions

Please review the following information before working the projects in this book. Important details about the abbreviations and symbols used are included.

Hooks

Crochet hooks are sized for different weights of yarn and thread. For thread crochet, you will usually use a steel crochet hook. Steel crochet hook sizes range from size 00 to 14. The higher the number of hook, the smaller your stitches will be. For example, a size 1 steel crochet hook will give you much larger stitches than a size 9 steel crochet hook.

Keep in mind that the sizes given with the pattern instructions were obtained by working with the size thread or yarn and hook given in the materials list. If you work with a smaller hook, depending on your gauge, your project size will be smaller; if you work with a larger hook, your finished project's size will be larger.

Gauge

Gauge is determined by the tightness or looseness of your stitches, and affects the finished size of your project. If you are concerned about the finished size of the project matching the size given, take time to crochet a small section of the pattern and then check your gauge. For example, if the gauge called for is 10 dc = 1 inch, and your gauge is 12 dc to the inch, you should switch to a larger hook. On the other hand, if your gauge is only 8 dc to the inch, you should switch to a smaller hook.

If the gauge given in the pattern is for an entire motif, work one motif and then check your gauge.

Understanding Symbols

As you work through a pattern, you'll quickly notice several symbols in the instructions. These symbols are used to clarify the pattern for you: Brackets [], curlicue brackets {}, asterisks *.

Brackets [] are used to set off a group of instructions worked a number of times. For example, "[ch 3, sc in ch-3 sp] 7 times" means to work the instructions inside the [] seven times. Brackets [] also set off a group of stitches to be worked in one stitch, space or loop. For example, the brackets [] in this set of instructions, "Sk 3 sc, [3 dc, ch 1, 3 dc] in next st" indicate that after skipping 3 sc, you will work 3 dc, ch 1 and 3 more dc all in the next stitch.

Occasionally, a set of instructions inside a set of brackets needs to be repeated, too. In this case, the text within the brackets to be repeated will be set off with curlicue brackets {}. For example, "[Ch 9, yo twice, insert hook in 7th ch from hook and pull up a loop, sk next dc, yo, insert hook in next dc and pull up a loop, {yo and draw through 2 lps on hook} 5 times, ch 3] 8 times." In this case, in each of the eight times you work the instructions included in brackets, you will work the section included in curlicue brackets five times.

Asterisks * are also used when a group of instructions is repeated. They may either be used alone or with brackets. For example, "*Sc in each of the next 5 sc, 2 sc in next sc, rep from * around, join with a sl st in beg sc" simply means you will work the instructions from the first * around the entire round.

"*Sk 3 sc, [3 dc, ch 1, 3 dc] in next st, rep from * around" is an example of asterisks working with brackets. In this set of instructions, you will repeat the instructions from the asterisk around, working the instructions inside the brackets together. ★

Buyer's Guide

When looking for a specific material, first check your local craft stores and yarn shops. If you are unable to locate a product, contact the manufacturers listed below for the closest retail source in your area.

Caron International
P.O. Box 222
Washington, NC 27889
(800) 868-9194

Coats & Clark
Consumer Service,
P.O. Box 12229,
Greenville, SC 26912-0229
(800) 648-1479

Elmore-Pisgah Inc.
P.O. Box 187
Springdale, NC 28160
(800) 633-7829

Lion Brand Yarn Co.
34 W. 15th St.,
New York, NY 10011
(800) 795-5466

STITCH GUIDE

Front Loop (a)
Back Loop (b)

Chain (ch)
Yo, draw lp through hook.

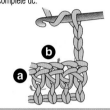

Slip Stitch Joining
Insert hook in beg ch, yo, draw lp through.

Front Post/Back Post Dc
Fpdc (a): Yo, insert hook from front to back and to front again around the vertical post (upright part) of next st, yo and draw yarn through, yo and complete dc.
Bpdc (b): Yo, reaching over top of piece and working on opposite side (back) of work, insert hook from back to front to back again around vertical post of next st, yo and draw yarn through, yo and complete dc.

Single Crochet (sc)
Insert hook in st (a), yo, draw lp through (b), yo, draw through both lps on hook (c).

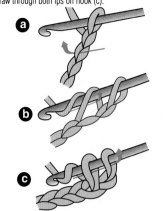

Half-Double Crochet (hdc)
Yo, insert hook in st (a), yo, draw lp through (b), yo, draw through all 3 lps on hook (c).

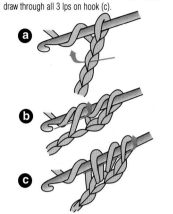

DECREASING

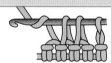

Single Crochet Decrease
Dec 1 sc over next 2 sts as follows: Draw up a lp in each of next 2 sts, yo, draw through all 3 lps on hook.

Double Crochet Decrease
Dec 1 dc over next 2 sts as follows: [Yo, insert hook in next st, yo, draw up lp on hook, yo, draw through 2 lps] twice, yo, draw through all 3 lps on hook.

Double Crochet (dc)
Yo, insert hook in st (a), yo, draw lp through (b), [yo, draw through 2 lps] twice (c, d).

Treble Crochet (tr)
Yo hook twice, insert hook in st (a), yo, draw lp through (b), [yo, draw through 2 lps on hook] 3 times (c, d, e).

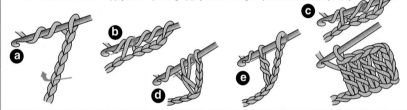

SPECIAL STITCHES

Chain Color Change (ch color change)
Yo with new color, draw through last lp on hook.

Double Crochet Color Change (dc color change)
Drop first color, yo with new color, draw through last 2 lps of st.

Reverse Single Crochet (reverse sc)
Working from left to right, insert hook in next st to the right (a), yo, draw up lp on hook, complete as for sc (b).

Stitch Abbreviations
The following stitch abbreviations are used throughout this publication.

beg	begin(ning)
bl(s)	block(s)
bpdc	back post dc
ch(s)	chain(s)
cl(s)	cluster(s)
CC	contrasting color
dc	double crochet
dec	decrease
dtr	double treble crochet
fpdc	front post dc
hdc	half-double crochet
inc	increase
lp(s)	loop(s)
MC	main color
p	picot
rem	remain(ing)
rep	repeat
rnd(s)	round(s)
RS	right side facing you
sc	single crochet
sk	skip
sl st	slip stitch
sp(s)	space(s)
st(s)	stitch(es)
tog	together
tr	treble crochet
trtr	triple treble crochet
WS	wrong side facing you
yo	yarn over

Crochet Hooks

METRIC	US
.60mm	14 steel
.75mm	12 steel
1.00mm	10 steel
1.25mm	8 steel
1.50mm	7 steel
1.75mm	5 steel
2.00mm	B/1
2.50mm	C/2
3.00mm	D/3
3.50mm	E/4
4.00mm	F/5
4.50mm	G/6
5.00mm	H/8
5.50mm	I/9
6.00mm	J/10

Yarn Conversion
OUNCES TO GRAMS

1	28.4
2	56.7
3	85.0
4	113.4

GRAMS TO OUNCES

25	7⁄8
40	1 2⁄5
50	1 3⁄4
100	3 1⁄2

Crochet Abbreviations

US	INTL
sc—single crochet	dc—double crochet
dc—double crochet	tr—treble crochet
hdc—half-double crochet	htr—half treble crochet
tr—treble crochet	dtr—double treble crochet
dtr—double treble crochet	trip—triple treble crochet
sk—skip	miss

YARNS

Bedspread weight	No. 10 cotton or Virtuoso
Sport weight	3-ply or thin DK
Worsted weight	Thick DK or Aran

Check tension or gauge to save time.

Special Thanks

We'd like to thank the following crochet designers whose work is featured in this collection of afghans. We appreciate their ongoing effort to create unique and beautiful crochet patterns.

Sandra Abbate
Festive Pine & Holly, Pineapple Promise

Eleanor Albano-Miles
Bobbles & Squares Delight, Christmas Home, Santa Fe Panels, Desert Medallions

Carol Alexander
Spring Bouquets

Sue Childress
Pretty Popcorns

Kathryn Clark
Painted Daisies

Rosalie DeVries
Pueblo Vistas

Dot Drake
Floral Parade, Flower Cart, Paneled Throw, Pastel Scrap Delight

Jo Hanna Dzikowski
Golden Harvest Cables

Katherine Eng
American Pride, Saguaro Print

Darla Fanton
All-American Plaid, Baby's Reversible Ripples, Colorful Bricks, Country Roses, Dream Puff Delight, Jeweled Bobbles, Raspberry Shells, Surf & Sand

Kathleen Garen
Chocolate Layer Cake, Log Cabin Comfort

Laura Gebhardt
Country Estate

Anne Halliday
Indian Gold, Sunny Days

Tammy Hildebrand
Blue Cables, Christmas Crosses, Kaleidoscope Vista, Painted Stripes, Rainbow Ripple, Springtime Shells, Stained Glass Motifs, Winter Wheat, Yo-Yo Strips

Theresa Jones
Floral Fantasy

Melissa Leapman
Fields of Corn, Lacy Shells, Simple Shells (Confetti Shells and Sunny Shells), Wavy Shells

Darla McGuire
Country Hearts & Roses

Carolyn Pfeifer
City Blocks

Diane Poellot
Argyle & Cables, Diagonal Tiles, Diamond Rosebud, Twist Stitch Stripes

Josie Rabier
Lacy Delight

Agnes Russell
Stadium Blanket

Barbara Shaffer
Navajo Blanket

Ruth Shepherd
Warm Your Heart

Martha Brooks Stein
Cheerful Cherries, Country Checks & Hearts, Summer Picnic

Angela Tate
Tasseled Motifs, Textured Aran

Maggie Weldon
Desert Sky, Diamond Strip

Notes